The New
Merger Game

Also by Don Gussow

Divorce Corporate Style

The New Merger Game

The Plan and the Players

DON GUSSOW

amacom

A Division of
American Management Associations

Ro⸱   ⸱ier **Library**

JUN 28 1978

Tallahassee, Florida

Library of Congress Cataloging in Publication Data

Gussow, Don.
   The new merger game.

   Includes index.
   1. Consolidation and merger of corporations.
I. Title.
HD2741.G87   338.8   77-28480
ISBN 0-8144-5463-1

First Printing

For Marvin Toben, who has experienced, with me, a merger and a buyback.

Preface

THIS BOOK DEALS WITH the merger game as it is played now—and in all likelihood will be played into the eighties. A large part of the book is case histories of good and bad mergers, and of founders and other executives of merged companies who have made it with their new corporate parents. Much is drawn from my own experience and close observation as business reporter, writer, and editor. Since the Great Depression I have been part of the American business scene, observing and reporting on the unique facet of mergers and acquisitions. In fact I was involved in one myself. In 1966 I sold the company I founded and controlled to a large and prestigious public communications empire, serving on its board of directors and holding the position of divisional president. During the next three and a half years I watched as my colleagues acquired several companies for our parent corporation, and I personally acquired several more. In 1970 I bought back my original company and some of the companies I had acquired for the corporation.

This book is written largely for the successful independent entrepreneur who may be interested in selling his company to a public corporation. I have, however, tried to include information for just about any business executive, as well as for bankers, accountants, corporation lawyers, the investment community, even people in academia who specialize in the economics and methodology of industry and business.

Although not intended as a text, the book does discuss the legal and accounting aspects of mergers or acquisitions, together with tax options attendant upon various merger and acquisition situations.

We hope the book will enable the student of business to learn much more about the new merger game and its implications. For the independent entrepreneur (and his family, his associates, and his employees), it could be of special interest and value, if it helps him make sound decisions in playing the merger and acquisition game.

For their help and counsel in writing this book I particularly wish to thank: Ira Sheinfeld and Robert N. Waxman of J. K. Lasser & Company, certified public accountants (which was merged into Touche Ross & Co. on August 20, 1977), who provided valuable technical information relating to accounting and tax matters of merger situations; David Regosin of Regosin, Edwards, Freeman & Stone, attorneys, who guided me on legal, estate planning, and lawyer-client aspects in mergers and acquisitions; Herbert Tenzer and Benjamin Raphan of

Tenzer, Greenblatt, Fallon & Kaplan, attorneys, who assisted on matters relating to the position of the Securities and Exchange Commission in mergers and acquisitions, and with technical data on other legal matters; Stanley Foster Reed, editor and publisher of the quarterly publication *Mergers and Acquisitions*, one of the most informed people in the merger area, who added considerably to my knowledge and understanding of sophisticated merger and acquisition transactions; Willard Grimm, president of W. T. Grimm & Co., who has been widely quoted on the subject of mergers and who gave me substantial statistical and technical merger and acquisition data; and finally the chairmen, presidents, and other corporate executives throughout industry whose firsthand experiences with mergers and acquisitions were indispensable.

DON GUSSOW
New York
January 1978

Contents

CONTENTS

Upfront One

Introducing the New Merger Game

FEW THINGS IN BUSINESS are more exciting, stimulating, or exhilarating than the merger game. For the millions who experience it directly or indirectly, the merger or acquisition process *is* a game, not always a fun game but a game nonetheless. It has its players and special rules, its winners and losers. As in all games, the rules change as times and needs change.

The merger game has been played throughout the history of business, but it began getting manic during the so-called go-go sixties, peaking in 1969. Those were the days—especially from 1965 through 1968—when just about any privately owned company, with or without a record of growth and profitability, could have been sold. Many were, in some instances at outrageous prices. Most of these companies were acquired by would-be conglom-

1

erates that went public just for that purpose—to grow through acquisition and the use of leverage. They bought companies with their stock, sometimes called "funny money," and they could do it because during these go-go years their paper was selling at excessively high price/earnings ratios. With their stock going at 30 to 40 times earnings or higher, some acquiring companies were able to buy other companies at prices approaching their own multiples. Sometimes the going price for an acquired company was even greater. Buying for "potential growth" was the rationale they used.

This type of activity went by the boards beginning in late 1970, reaching the end of the line in the recession period of 1974 and early 1975. Then, listed stock (some issued by the nation's most prestigious corporations) was selling at less than ten times earnings—often at multiples as low as five, four, or even three. But even under such trying circumstances the merger game did not end. Acquisitions continued, only now usually for cash rather than stock, or by other forms of paper such as preferreds and debentures.

Thus, although about 7,000 mergers were completed in 1968, fewer than 3,000 corporate marriages were consummated in 1974, the fewest in more than 15 years. The picture was no better in 1975 or early in 1976. Beginning with the second quarter of 1976, however, as the recession waned and earning multiples of public stock began to show a meaningful reversal upward, the merger game started to generate new excitement and activity.

At this writing—late 1977—the investment banking

community continues to believe that the merger and acquisition ways of the sixties are gone forever. Maybe so, but forever is a very long time. Besides, history does have a way of repeating itself, in a different form. Consequently, there is no way to know at this time what vogue, rage, craze, hue, or adaptation the merger game will assume at the end of the seventies and in the early eighties. But one thing seems certain. The game will be with us and could very well accelerate in the years ahead. A new era of mergers and acquisitions is already developing on the business horizon, and with it a new kind of game, new in many ways and approaches. One is the greater use of cash instead of securities—especially by cash-rich corporations whose stock still sells at low or moderately low price/earnings multiples. Also part of the new game is learning how to adjust to changes required by the Tax Reform Act of 1976. In evidence again too are "raiding" and "takeover" bids, with arbitrageurs active. Not an innovative approach but one dormant since 1968, arbitraging began to pick up in the mid-seventies, and in the hot summer of 1977 it was flourishing.

An interesting case is the purchase of Cannon Mills Co. stock by Gulf + Western Industries, Inc. Headed by the brilliant, tough, almost legendary conglomerator Charles Bluhdorn, G + W—a $3 billion or so corporation diversified into such things as zinc, candy, movies, books, oil, and insurance operations—has aquired more than a hundred companies since its founding in 1958, not a few through the raiding and takeover bid strategy. With the stock of the famous Atlanta-based bedding company selling at around $13 a share, $10 less than book value, Gulf + Western began to buy. By the time G + W accumulated 4 percent of Cannon stock, the price was close to $23, just about book value, but still less than its 1972 high of $42 a share. With Cannon's insiders holding 20 percent of the company's stock, G + W was in a fair position, at least, for a takeover bid. In June 1976 Mr. Bluhdorn mailed a letter to Chairman and CEO Harold P. Hornaday of Cannon advising him that G + W was "interested" in increasing its position in Cannon. G + W would do this by way of a tender offer for 1.5 million Cannon Mills shares in exchange for approximately $50 million of G + W debentures. As Mr. Bluhdorn "explained" it to Cannon's boss man, the acquisition of the Cannon Mills's stock was "for investment purposes only."

Although the Cannon management had not liked it, it had been able to accommodate itself to G + W's 4 percent interest. (Not that it was given much choice; the stock had been acquired in the "normal" manner over a long period of time.) But 1.5 million additional shares, giving G + W a 20 percent interest in Cannon, was something else. Thus, Cannon's board moved quickly, voting to repurchase G + W's 4 percent or 362,800 shares. It offered G + W $8 million—$22 a share. Bluhdorn accepted the proposition. It gave his company a substantial capital gain in the fairly short period of about a year. By the end of 1976 the deal was completed.

Although G + W did not succeed in its Cannon takeover attempt, it still follows this approach in efforts to acquire other firms, or to "invest" in such corporations by (not so quietly) buying their stock on the open market. A good example is the acquisition over a period of time of the stock of Esquire, Inc., publishers of *Esquire* magazine but owners of various other businesses, such as the manufacture and importation of electric bulbs. G + W already owns about 25 percent of Esquire stock, which went from a low of $4 a share to as high as $12, with arbitrageurs making a killing as G + W began to acquire it. (Early in September 1977, *Esquire* magazine was sold to former founder/publisher of *New York* magazine Clay Felker, Milton Glazer, and Vere Harmsworth, British newspaper publisher.)

When Esmark, Inc. moved to acquire Inmont Corp. early in 1977 (Inmont was eventually acquired by Carrier Corp.), Inmont's stock rose quickly from a low of $16 to $22 per share (and seems to be going higher). Again, arbitrageurs are profiting. More activity like this on the domestic merger and acquisition front can be expected in the months and possibly years ahead—unless federal and state legislatures move to restrict or stop it, a doubtful happening although anything is possible.

In the meantime, raiding or takeover bids, having accelerated to a marked degree since 1976, continue. With the stock of so many good companies still selling at below book value, famous corporate raiders prowl about, quietly buying it up on the open market. When the corporate raider accumulates a sizable position in a company he moves in with a takeover bid.

This is becoming so widespread that scarcely a week

passes without some public company finding itself needing to defend its "integrity" against a "raid." This usually happens to companies whose management, including the board of directors, lacks enough stock to keep strong working control over their enterprise. This may vary from 5 to 20 percent, depending on the size of the company and the number of shares issued and outstanding. Corporations whose stock is selling at a price considerably less than book value, with a strong cash position but a lackluster growth record, are prime targets for takeover bids, and a high percentage of these "creeping takeovers," in the language of Wall Street, succeed.

More evidence that the merger game is about to return vigorously in the near future is the new flurry of companies "going public." During March 1976 alone, eight companies completed or announced initial public offerings of their securities, as many as in all 1975. Since then, several public issues have been completed each week, as attested to by the increasing number of tombstone ads in *The Wall Street Journal*. Going public is again in style. Underwriters are again on the prowl for privately owned companies with good earning and growth records, prime candidates for "going public." We are also beginning to see more public companies buying their own stock on the open market, especially when the stock is undervalued and can be used later to acquire other companies. Both activities are bound to speed up the interest in mergers and acquisitions.

Until the mid-seventies, the fast-moving corporations, usually active in conglomerating, shied away from much merger and acquisition involvement. Now we are beginning to see new interest and even some activity here. As the price of the conglomerates' stock rises, we are bound to see more, but the most active buyers of businesses today are the established, seasoned, financially strong, sometimes cash-rich corporations. The management of these companies knows that the best way to grow aggressively and substantially is through a sound merger and acquisition program. These old-line firms are especially interested in buying companies that are congeneric—that is, in the same or related lines of business. With some exceptions, a food company will no longer be interested in a girdle maker, a shoe manufacturing operation, or a metal fabricator. What the food company usually wants is another food company, but one with a different corporate concept, perhaps, or with a product line that fits its own marketing and distribution setup.

We see this in the acquisition of Riviana Foods Inc. by the Colgate-Palmolive Co. With annual sales at the time of the merger of just under $2.5 billion and net earnings of just under $120 million, Colgate acquired Riviana, whose annual sales as of June 1976 were below $500 million and whose earnings were just under $12 million, by an exchange of Colgate-Palmolive stock, valued at slightly over $172 million. C-P, an old-line company, is a worldwide producer and marketer of consumer goods, largely in proprietary and ethical health-care items and cosmetics. Riviana, a fast-growing Houston-based operation, processes and distributes

Mexican-style rice and rice products and kosher processed meat products as well as other foods. This acquisition brings Colgate-Palmolive into a type of food business congeneric with its basic line of household and proprietary merchandise.

As a result of this and another acquisition (the Charles A. Eaton Co., producer and marketer of sports footwear congeneric with C-P's Leisure and Entertainment Division), Colgate-Palmolive wound up 1976 with sales better than $3.5 billion and net income just under $150 million. Its goal is $5 billion in annual sales with net earnings of $250 million or better. This is the type of merger and acquisition program that is being followed by an increasingly large number of public corporations whose aim is continual, constructive growth. More of this activity can be expected before the seventies end.

We are also beginning to see a few acquisitions by smaller public companies, some listed on the American Stock Exchange and over the counter. These successful medium-size operations, with single or limited product or service lines, want to broaden their product and marketing bases. We foresee more of this type of merger and acquisition, particularly in 1978, if the economy continues to improve.

Also observed at this time is the unusual interest by European and other foreign companies in acquiring American enterprises. Their reasons are pragmatic. They feel that from the long-range view, the American economy is the world's strongest. Ditto for the dollar, compared with European and other foreign currencies. We have also noticed a new and unique twist. Foreign managements, especially in Europe, see socialism taking over a good part of the world— throughout Europe, in Latin America, in Africa, and in most of Asia. They feel that eventually the United States will embrace socialism too. However, they reason that our economy will remain the last bulwark of capitalism—at least for the next 50 years, perhaps longer. Thus, they have decided that investment in American business is a much safer gamble than investment elsewhere. As a result, the larger firms of Italy, England, the Netherlands, Sweden, and West Germany are exploring opportunities to buy American companies, or to settle for a minority position therein.

For example, the $3.5 billion W. R. Grace & Co. of New York, a major producer of chemicals, sold 4 million shares of newly issued stock, plus 265,660 outstanding shares, to the Flick Group of Düsseldorf, West Germany. This represents 12 percent of the outstanding Grace stock, giving the large West German combine a strong position in this interesting, growing American company. Indian Head Inc., the textile and glass manufacturing company with annual sales in excess of $400 million, sold a controlling interest last year to Holland's Thyssen-Bornemisza. These are only two examples of a trend that is expected to hasten in the years ahead.

Do fashions change in the new merger game? Interestingly, yes. At certain times, certain types of companies, industries, or special fields become more attractive than at other times, often for no particular reason. In 1976 and so far in 1977, two areas that have dominated the interest of company acquisitors have been energy and media.

Energy is definitely tied to the special needs of our time. Young, creative, high-technology firms involved in just about any phase of energy production—from coal to solar, including their allied equipment and instrumentation—have been and continue to be takeover targets for large, well-financed corporations. Or, lacking the capital to realize their own growth potential, some of these energy outfits go willingly into mergers with cash-rich corporations.

It is also interesting that many of the larger corporations have discovered it is less risky to invest $100 million or more ready cash or bank credit to buy an existing company with good plant facilities than to develop new products or additions themselves. This is because it is easier to evaluate the market potential for existing products than to introduce new, untried items, and because, as a result of inflation (which no doubt will continue), the cost of adding new plant and equipment is becoming excessive.

Then too, special problems now face companies that must adjust to new laws and regulations relating to the environment. The management of these companies has found it is less costly and less time consuming to buy existing facilities that already meet environmental standards than to invest in impact studies and then build new plants that satisfy such requirements.

However, the burgeoning activity of mergers and acquisitions in media during the past few years shows no specific rationale. Why would the Pritzker family of Chicago, involved in a variety of business investments, the most famous of which is the Hyatt chain of hotels, buy the long-floundering McCall Co., publishers of *McCall's* and *Redbook?* The official answer at the time of the acquisition: interesting growth and profit potential. There could be other reasons, such as the cultural and communication involvement such a merger might produce, but it is also a fact that the Pritzkers, sound investors and management oriented, are not likely to buy anything unless it has clear profit potential.

Most media mergers and acquisitions have been intraindustry, however, and often do show some rationale. CBS bought the Fawcett Publishing operation for about $50 million to strengthen its own not wholly successful publishing division. The New York Times Company added to its string of small newspapers (at this writing thirteen, ten in Florida and three in North Carolina) to diversify growth potential in an area it knows well. S. I. Newhouse, one of the nation's larger publishing empires (certainly the biggest in number of newspapers owned), bought Booth Newspapers, Inc., the Michigan chain of dailies, for more than $300 million in cash. (This, incidentally, started as an "unfriendly" takeover bid.)

The interest in media during the past few years has centered on newspapers and specialized consumer magazines, with particular emphasis on periodicals covering such sporting activities as golf, tennis, and boating.

As of this writing, the buying activity in business and professional magazines is fairly quiet, but that could change toward the end of the seventies. Some beginnings are here, as evidenced by the acquisition (at the end of 1977) of the Technical Publishing Co., Barrington, Illinois (OTC) by Dun & Bradstreet, Inc., for $45 million of its stock. Earlier, Pittway Corporation (American Exchange) bought Penton, Inc., an old-time business magazine company of Cleveland, and merged it into its own Industrial Publishing Co., also of Cleveland, to form Penton/IPC, Inc. This field matured during the past decade, is still growing, and offers substantial profit potential and further growth.

Some other trends? Buying for cash, by cash-rich corporations and by those who can enrich their treasuries through secondary public stock offerings, will continue in the foreseeable future. At the same time, as stock prices rise, selling for stock should return. It is starting now. With the tightening of long-term capital gains treatment by the Tax Reform Act of 1976, sellers are beginning to prefer to take—and hold—stock of seasoned, financially strong public corporations, especially if they yield good or at least moderate dividends. Capital gains taxes need not be paid unless, and until, the stock or the portion acquired in a merger transaction is sold.

Thus far, public companies in the market for privately owned firms appear to be selective. The prices they offer are on the modest side, certainly more modest than prices they paid in the soaring sixties. Ten times net earnings seems the going rate in early 1978, but it could soon change dramatically if the demand for acquisitions increases. In mid-1977 there was a moderate backlog of selling companies. This pool is beginning to evaporate, and when it's gone, prices are bound to rise. Even in the merger and acquisition game, it is a matter of supply and demand.

Upfront Two

Defining a Merger

OF COURSE *you* know what a merger is, but have you ever asked other business people to define it? Try and you will probably be amazed. Ask a lawyer or an accountant to define "merger" and you will be in real trouble. Look it up in the dictionary. The definition you find will depend on the dictionary you use.

I started with *Webster's Third New International Dictionary* (unabridged)—the one our writers and editors use, the big one. These are the first four definitions I found under "merge": "(1) to plunge or engulf in a medium that wholly surrounds or absorbs: immerse; (2) to cause to be legally absorbed, sunk, or extinguished by merger; (3) to cause to combine, unite, or coalesce (planned to *merge* two companies); (4) to blend gradually; alter by transitional stages; blunt or destroy the distinctiveness of (individuality and uniqueness are *merged* and blurred)."

But there were others too. Then, among the definitions of "merger" in the same dictionary, I found two that are especially applicable: "absorption by a corporation of one or more others," and "any of various other methods of combining two or more business concerns."

Because I still felt I had not pinpointed it precisely enough, I also went to *The Random House Dictionary of the English Language* (one of the newest) and to my old desk companion, the *Thorndike-Barnhart Comprehensive Desk Dictionary*. According to *The Random House Dictionary*, "merge" means "(1) to cause to combine or coalesce; unite; (2) to combine, blend, or unite gradually so as to blur the individuality of (often followed by in to into); (3) to become combined, united, swallowed up, or absorbed . . . ; (4) to combine or unite into a single enterprise. . . ." Under "merger": "(1) a statutory combination of two or more corporations by the transfer of the properties to one surviving corporation; (2) any combination of two or more business enterprises into a single enterprise"—and so on.

Turning to *Thorndike-Barnhart* I found " 'merge': (1) swallow up, absorb, combine, and absorb, combine; (2) become swallowed up or combined in something else." Under "merger": "a merging, absorption, combination: ('one big company was formed by the merger of four small ones.')."

So much for definitions from three dictionaries.

I next went to the 559-page *Anatomy of a Merger* by James C. Freund (The Law Journal Press, 1975). Here I found not a definition but a maze—no single definition

15

but a list of descriptions of and discussions on various "combinations" and their structures.

Under the subhead "An Ode to Structuring" in his lengthy chapter on "Structuring the Transaction," the author, a Princeton University and Harvard Law School graduate and partner in the New York law firm of Skadden, Arps, Slate, Meagher & Flom, says:

> The plain fact is that there is virtually no legal transaction that can be quite so complex and multidisciplined as a business combination (i.e., merger). And the point at which it all comes together (or falls apart) is in structuring the transaction . . . (i.e., of the merger or combination). For the acquisition lawyer, the most stimulating aspect of the deal from an intellectual point of view is the structuring.

A short, enlightening paragraph from the same chapter, same book, states:

> We begin with the premise that the object of the typical acquisition transaction is for the business that was formerly operated by T to come to rest in P, or in a wholly owned subsidiary of P. From a mechanical, corporate point of view, this can be accomplished in various ways.

Elsewhere in this chapter the author explains these ways, and in doing so he lays out almost endlessly the forms mergers can take. Designed for lawyers who specialize in mergers and acquisitions, Freund's book gets extremely detailed. He deals with the legal, not corporate, strategies and techniques for negotiating acquisitions, and thus gives us a game plan for lawyers, emphasizing the negotiating process. Says Mr. Freund: "To call off a deal is no trouble at all, but it requires some real ability to hold together the pieces of a difficult acquisition and accomplish it in a way that satisfies all parties."

Although some merger transactions are more difficult than others, my own experience, observation, and research suggest that there is no such thing as an easy acquisition. The problems and situations that often arise are complicated and practically interminable.

Still, because mergers will continue to be a way of business life for as long as we can forsee, the more business people know about them, the better they will cope with the personal and management problems they involve. At one time or another just about every corporation will experience these transactions directly or indirectly, and so will their managers. What then is the correct, most meaningful, or at least the most useful definition of a merger? Mine is: A merger is the combining of one company with another, or the absorption or blending of one company into another.

Interestingly, the phrase "swallow up" is found in most dictionary definitions. The question we must ask, and which we touch upon later, is this: Is the smaller company, the one that is merged into or acquired by a larger corporation, usually swallowed by it and somehow destroyed? Equally important, does it have to be?

Quick answers to both questions are yes, some acquired smaller companies are swallowed, but no, they do not have to be. Very often they are not. Without exception, the managements of the acquiring corporations do not want the smaller company to be swallowed up. Anything that risks stunting the acquired company's growth potential and limiting the effectiveness of its management would be counterproductive. To begin with, rarely will a company buy another that lacks management.

Which brings us to the more human or personal considerations. Certainly a merger is a combining of companies, plants, facilities, products—but it is also the melding of people. In a merger, as in almost every human activity, the people element is paramount. In fact, it could well be the single most important determinant of a merger's success or failure. Unless a working affinity between the groups of people on both sides can be established, and established quickly, the merger will not succeed. Terms and goals must be clearly defined and established at the outset. The people most directly involved in the merger must be compatible. They must empathize with one another and understand not only the merger program itself but also its various implications. Then and only then will there be a solid base for a successful merger or business combination, dictionary definitions aside.

What it may all come down to is what the buyer looks for in the seller: profitability, market share, growth potential, and capable management, with the buyer supplying only the capital for growth and overall supervision.

If the purpose of just about any acquisition is profitable growth, the only ways for the buyer to attain it are by increasing the sale or market share of existing products and services, or by introducing new ones. Often the

easiest, most effective way of doing this is to buy someone else's.

It does not always work out this way, obviously, despite all good intentions and planning. Thus there are
good and bad mergers, buybacks and spin-offs of acquired companies, and other disposals. The record of
merger transactions has its share of disasters, but the
point is still this: Without a sound, well-developed program of mergers and acquisitions, no company whose
goal is steady growth, and certainly no public corporation, could achieve its goal fully.

So again let me emphasize that mergers have been
and will continue to be a way of life of our economic
system. Game plans may change with the times and conditions, but mergers and acquisitions themselves will
persist. They are as vital to corporate growth as to efficient capital utilization. In the end, the reason for mergers and acquisitions may be the best definition of them.

Chapter

1

The Merger Game
Can Do Big Things

JIM WEISS STARTED his business in the forties with 60 cents. With that he acquired a broken-down mimeograph machine which he proceeded to put in working order. That done he launched a "printing" business with a staff of one—himself. He was printer, financial executive, and salesman. He was also purchasing agent, clerk, secretary, shipping department, delivery man, and artist, layout designer, advertising and promotion consultant. He had a few other titles and chores too.

Jim sold mimeo "printing" to local stores on the West Side of Chicago. As salesman and merchandiser he was good, but because he had no stencils, ink, or paper he would ask customers for an advance with each order. He was able to accomplish this almost impossible feat by promising—and delivering—copy and layouts "for free."

He got his supplies and in time had a profitable, growing mail-order printing business, specializing in church bulletins.

Now, although Jim was in his early twenties and had little formal education, he did have a goal. It was to build a business big enough and profitable enough, with sufficient growth potential, to merge with Beatrice Foods. Why merge? And why with Beatrice Foods? Jim may have lacked a degree but he was not an uneducated person. Although gifted and motivated, he could not enter college because he never finished high school. As a matter of fact, he was an elementary school dropout. His family's situation was such that at the age of nine he had to earn his own keep.

But Jim had studied at night and on weekends, particularly at the old Armour Institute, now the Illinois Institute of Technology. The courses he liked best were in engineering, economics, and business management. With his photographic memory and analytic mind, he learned well, and before long he could match wits with any Harvard MBA. After careful and scientific study, Jim concluded that if he ever owned a company or a piece of one, Beatrice Foods would be it. He liked its management, its business philosophy, its product mix, its program for expansion.

Jim's reasons for picking Beatrice as his eventual merger partner were well thought out and constructive. Beatrice had developed an ambitious and expansive long-range acquisition program, but it was a conservative company, the kind that would not be hell-bent to buy whatever came along. Jim's studies revealed that Beatrice would not buy a company that required venture capital for development. Instead it bought established, profitable operations with sound entrepreneurial management which it let run its own show, offering only paternal supervision and encouragement from above. Jim concluded that here was a corporation that would grow internally as well as through acquisition, one with a humane yet pragmatic business approach. He wanted stock in a growing public company, yet also an opportunity to expand his own horizon. Beatrice was for him.

With Beatrice in mind, Jim applied his direct marketing, advertising, and promotion experience to expand his basic operation. He started a unique, highly specialized candy company that made just one product, a peanut butter candy pillow, which he marketed exclusively to fund raisers. His connections with churches and other institutions made it practicable, and Jim succeeded beautifully. Soon he added a second line, chocolate bars that fund raisers could merchandise under their own or another label or trademark. Within six years, in 1965, Jim merged his Chesterton Candy Co. into Beatrice Foods for $6 million worth of Beatrice common stock. (It was that profitable!) At the same time he kept his original business, designing and printing church bulletins.

During the next few years several other interesting things happened to Jim. His Beatrice stock was now worth more than $10 million. The Beatrice management also began to appreciate his creative talents and operational skill, and soon utilized both in its own corporate development. Beatrice acquired Jim's printing company and before long Jim became president of the corporation's Educational and Consumer Arts Division. Now representing $400 million of Beatrice's almost $6 billion annual volume, it has one of the corporation's best records for sales and profit growth. In 1975, elected a Beatrice executive vice-president (one of five), Jim was also put in charge of the corporation's Chemical Division. With combined volume nearing $700 million, the potential is there for a billion-dollar operation before long. Now (1977) he is a member of the board of directors at a salary of $208,000 per year, although with incentives he could make much more. When he retires at 65, he will probably receive a pension in excess of $70,000 a year. His 400,000 shares (worth $25 each in 1977) make him Beatrice's largest single stockholder.

Not bad for a fellow who started his business with 60 cents. Assuredly, Jim Weiss deserves everything he now has. He is a brilliant, self-made entrepreneur who built a successful business, profitable enough for a firm like Beatrice to want to buy it. Most important, Jim was able to adjust to the needs of the corporation. In doing so, he proved a valuable executive who made, and should continue to make, a strong contribution to the growing Beatrice business.

Obviously this was a successful merger, both for the buyer and the seller, but before rushing off to sell your own business it would be best to think twice and perhaps three times. The fact is, Jim Weiss represents an excep-

23

tion. It is also true that there have been far too many merger disasters. Merged companies have been ruined, and hard-working, proud entrepreneurs have died in the process—the direct or indirect result of their frustrations and calamitous experiences.

Don't get me wrong. I am not opposed to mergers themselves. I love business, what business stands for, especially American business, and what it accomplishes for the world's economy and the well-being of our people, materially and socially and culturally. Without business we would have little or nothing, despite some familiar criticisms of the American industrial complex. American business has demonstrated positive leadership toward worthy economic ends, and without expansion—which must include merging and acquiring —business and our entire economy would soon atrophy.

But—and the qualification is significant—the merger game can be a dangerous undertaking. Thus, before we talk more about the rules of the game, we should first look at a few more case histories. Some are real horror stories. Others deal with the psychological impact the game has had on individuals such as Walter Koziol.

When Walter returned from World War II Marine service in 1946, he had a difficult time adjusting to civilian life. He was 25 and personable but possessed only a meager education, having left high school at the end of his first year. He did, however, have a mechanical bent. This, plus a natural ability to relate to people, made him a potentially skillful salesman. After traveling a bit to find himself, Walter returned to his home in Antioch,

Illinois. There he found a job selling for an appliance manufacturing company. He did well, establishing new sales records in his territory and making friends as he went along. In 1959, at age 38, he decided to go into business for himself. The manufacturer he worked for had high regard for his dependability as well as his talent, and granted Walter a distributorship for some of the company's products. Because of his creative mechanical and marketing approach, he was particularly successful selling outdoor gas lamps. This became his profitable specialty.

Two years later, in 1961, Walter formed the Charmglow Products Company and began to manufacture not only his own outdoor gas lamps but also outdoor gas grills. The business took off and Charmglow gas grills soon joined other top brands as a highly successful, widely selling barbecue cooker. Then Walter invited his two brothers into the business. During the several years that followed, Charmglow expanded and was able to make and market a complete line of outdoor gas cookers and accessories. As a result, offers to buy the company began to come in, and fast. In 1967, only six years after Charmglow became a manufacturer and only eight after he went independent, Walter Koziol sold his business—also to Beatrice Foods.

It was superb judgment and excellent timing. This was at the height of the go-go years. All kinds of conglomerates were bidding extraordinary prices for all types of companies. Walter was not about to get stuck with the stock of an unproved corporation, even if it offered more for his business than he might have gotten from the highly regarded, proven management of Beatrice. He exchanged all of the issued and outstanding stock of his three companies for 115,764 shares of Beatrice common. Beatrice also agreed to issue a maximum of 115,764 more common, the exact number depending upon the combined net earnings of Koziol's three companies for each of the fiscal years ending February 1968, 1969, and 1970. The transaction as of the closing date, August 21, 1967, was valued at $6,945,000. Not a bad deal for either party, considering that sales of Koziol's combined companies amounted to $5,635,003, with net income after taxes of $395,539. The price offered represented slightly under 20 times earnings. This was considered a conservative purchase in those days, and very conservative when we remember that some conglomerates paid 40 times earnings for some companies, often more.

Beatrice, on the other hand, felt that it was buying a solid, profitable company, in a specialized field, with considerable growth potential and good management. Its judgment proved right. Charmglow grew substantially under its new supervision, which encouraged Walter Koziol and his associates to maximize product development and increase market penetration, sales, and profits. Beatrice was at a point when its own growth was accelerating, particularly in areas outside the food industry. Its sales amounted to $900 million, and net earnings, $30 million. By the end of February 1977, net sales for the preceding fiscal year were $5.3 billion, with net earnings of $182.5 million, the best by far in its 79-year-long history.

For Walter Koziol, the merger appeared to be an excellent step in his own career. He was now a multimillionaire. He owned the stock and had the financial and management backing of a tremendous public corporation, with an efficient and enlightened management team, headed by the able and dedicated William Karnes. Since this was a stock-for-stock merger, it was tax-free. Walter (and other members of his family) did not have to pay capital gains taxes, unless and until they sold any or all of their Beatrice shares. And, since Beatrice stock was of the strong and defensive variety, with a good record of appreciation and healthy periodic splits, there appeared to be no urgency *to* sell in the foreseeable future. Moreover, although dividends were not large, they were satisfactory and increased with the years. It looked like it was to be nothing but roses ahead for Walter Koziol.

But that was not the way it worked out. At least not entirely. And this is the point of recording the story of Charmglow, its associated companies, and of the entrepreneur and unique personality who started it.

The story unfolded as I interviewed Walter in his new street-floor offices on Main Street in Antioch, Illinois, a midwestern city of about 4,000, on a Monday morning in May 1977. Walter had retired as president of Charmglow (and associated companies) two months earlier to begin a new career as manufacturing consultant with two brothers, also retired from his Beatrice division.

The week before, he had placed the following classified advertisement in *The Wall Street Journal:*

MANUFACTURING CONSULTANT. Will Improve Manufacturing Profits. No Fees or Front Money. Fees Paid From Percentage of Increased Profits. Walter Koziol, 909 Main Street, Antioch, Illinois, (312) 395-7270.

He said that he had already received a number of interesting replies, which he was following up.

Shirtsleeved, neat, moustached, informal, genial, and easy to be with, Walter looked much younger than his 56 years. Why did he retire so soon, since at Beatrice the mandatory retirement age is 65? He was restless, he said, and felt it was time to do some new things on his own. He made the point that the idea was his, and he expressed only the highest regard for the Beatrice management team and its treatment of him and his associates. He said he could not have asked for greater understanding of what he was trying to do in managing the business after the merger. I mentioned that it was my understanding that he had made some investments in real estate. He confirmed this, saying that they were in condominiums in Hawaii and that some had not panned out too well. Hadn't he suffered substantial losses in other real estate investments, funded by bank loans and secured by some of his Beatrice stock? He confirmed this too, calling it the result of bad professional advice from a person with whom he had been associated for seven years.

I asked Walter to tell me how he felt about his situation. His reply:

"After all, how much money does one need? Enough to do what you want to do. I am fortunate in having a wonderful and understanding wife, a son who is making it in the business world on his own and with whom we have an excellent relationship, and a lovely teenage daughter who is a real charmer. One thing you learn as you go along is how unimportant it is to amass a big fortune. At least, this is what I learned. I have the satisfaction of having built a sizable business, I saw it grow to new heights after the merger with Beatrice—and now I am excited about my new career as a manufacturing consultant."

As I took leave of our pleasant interview, Walter said: "If you are going to write about me and Charmglow, be sure to say something nice about Beatrice and its executive team. They're the greatest."

Walter Koziol's experience is not unique. It happened to others who had sold their businesses in those times. It is important to remember that toward the end of the sixties and early in the seventies, a lot of people were reputed to have made killings in high-flying real estate deals, including the now infamous REITs. Others, among them some large and prestigious banks, lost millions—maybe billions—in such alluring (but often lurid) investments. Individuals with the gambling instinct, who sold their businesses for $5 to $10 million hoping to make $100 million, ruined themselves in the attempt.

The point is, it is not how good a deal one makes when he sells his business to a public corporation, but what he does with the proceeds and what happens to him personally afterward. Walter Koziol came out of it fairly well but surprising things can happen, and have happened, to executives who suddenly discover they are multimillionaires. Many normal, hard-working entrepreneurs are not able to make a healthy adjustment to their wealth, as Koziol did, and some go haywire attempting to convert their gains into huge fortunes, killing themselves in the process.

Anyway, if Koziol's was basically a good merger, just imagine what a bad merger could do to someone.

C. (for Charles) Laury Bothoff was sitting pretty. He had the sweetest thing anyone could hope for. He was president, chief executive officer, and majority stockholder of Standard Rate & Data Service, Inc., Skokie, Illinois. It was a unique publishing business, consisting of several monthly periodicals filled with information on advertising rates, circulation, production, and other essential data for all types of other media—daily and weekly newspapers, consumer magazines, business and professional periodicals, radio, and TV. The SRDS "books," as they are called, had long been the bibles of the media they served. An advertising agency could not function without its SRDS book. SRDS was, and continues to be, an essential service for media buyers and others in every advertising agency, big or small. And SRDS has no competition. Now and then someone tried to produce a competing compendium but soon gave up.

SRDS was started by Laury's father, Walter, in 1919. At 82, Walter was widely honored for his achievements in the field of media information and for his leadership, although it had been some years since his son and namesake had taken the helm. The founder was pleased with the job his son was doing. He had discovered a nice gold mine and his son not only cherished it but worked it well himself, expanding the operation in an intelligent and conservative manner.

By the late sixties, SRDS was at its peak. Construction was completed on a charming, exceptionally well designed headquarters building in Evanston. Laury had a large, smartly furnished office and the entire operation was now efficiently housed. Except for some important paintings in Laury's office, in those of several other executives, and in the lobby and public halls, it looked like what it was—a business building—but one done in excellent taste. The company continued to grow and prosper. It now also owned the National Register Publishing Co., Inc., publishers of such directories as the Standard Directory of Advertisers and the Standard Directory of Advertising Agencies. These basically were listings of major corporation advertisers and their agencies, cross indexed. Published annually and updated monthly, all were operating profitably—so profitably, in fact, that it was not long before the merger frenzy hit SRDS with a bang.

Laury Bothoff, just turned 50, well groomed, fit, and happily married to his beautiful second wife, began getting offers galore. They came from conglomerates and synergists, from brokers, directly from company chief executives, and from all sorts of different businesses. In those days, food companies were buying truck body firms, chemical concerns were adding retail stores, publishers were buying furniture makers. Everything seemed to go with anything, so long as the marriage partner was willing. Nor did the price really matter. The buyers gave paper—"Chinese money," as some called it.

Laury was tempted. He was now living like a millionaire, but the idea of being one proved overwhelming. What he apparently did not realize was that in the process he could lose his independence. More important, the millions he could receive would be in the form of paper. Still, if the paper was marketable stock of a big-board company, it could be worth more (as the stock appreciated with time and in possible stock splits) than inflation-prone currency. Or so he reasoned.

The company that succeeded in selling the merger idea to Laury was Macmillan, Inc., the New York based publishing conglomerate. Besides its diversified publishing operation, Macmillan, risen from the ashes of a once prestigious weekly magazine. *Collier's,* now owned a ragout of unrelated businesses. What impressed Laury was that among them was the highly regarded Brentano chain of bookstores, and Gump's of San Francisco, an interesting retail gift, art, and specialty store. Laury was also impressed by Macmillan's record of speedy growth and by its stock that kept pace going up. What he may not have known was that Macmillan's rise, particularly in its stock price, had a lot to do with leverage, a situation not uncommon among fast-track, acquisitive public companies of the sixties. In other words, Macmillan had no internal growth record of any consequence. It grew largely through acquisition, and to keep acquiring it had to borrow money from banks or institutional investors, continue to issue stock, and utilize a variety of accounting techniques, including pooling of interest. Not unlike other corporations those days, Macmillan lacked a rock-ribbed financial foundation.

Nevertheless, in 1969 Laury Bothoff's Standard Rate & Data Service was merged for $16 million of Macmillan's stock, at that time selling at $33 a share for a multiple close to 40. And, curious as it may seem for an astute businessman like Laury, he took letter stock, meaning that he could not sell any of it without Macmillan's permission and only then under a long list of other restrictions.

At least at the beginning, Laury was happy. He was now a multimillionaire, albeit of questionable paper, and president of an important division of an expanding *Fortune* 500 public company. Surely within five years his stock would double in value to $32 million or more—possibly to $50 million. Great, absolutely great.

Then came Laury's and his key executives' day of reckoning.

Within a year after the merger, Macmillan's stock began to tumble, soon reaching a low of $3 a share. At less than one-tenth the value it had when the merger was completed, Walter's stock was now worth about $1.6 million, not $16 million. (In 1977, the stock rebounded to $9 per share, increasing his holdings to about $4 million, but still only a quarter of what they once were.) Although this was not unusual for those who sold their businesses to conglomerates in the late sixties, it was no comfort to Laury. Hearkbroken, he flagellated himself for selling his business at all, and particularly to Macmillan. Barred from selling his letter stock in the $20 to $30 range, he felt it made no sense to sell any or a large part of it at $3 to $5, nor even at $9 a share, even if Macmillan let him. Actually, like partners in other mergers, Laury could have avoided some of the problem. His contract with Macmillan could have included a clause protecting against downside risk. He could have insisted on a bottom price of Macmillan stock, say $20 per share, so that if the price reached that point or went below, he would get additional stock to cover the difference between it and the price quoted on the New York Stock Exchange.

The sharp decline of his holdings was not the worst thing that happened to Laury, however. With its stock selling at about five times earnings, Macmillan lost its leverage. It could no longer buy other companies—particularly profitable ones—unless it paid for them with cash. But its cash position was low. This called for bank borrowings at continually increasing rates of interest, which made earnings slide. Too, some of Macmillan's acquisitions turned sour, resulting in heavy losses. Instead of buying it sought to divest, but buyers for losing operations were now practically nonexistent. The alternative was to take write-offs.

The fact is, Macmillan's chairman Ray Hagel was a giant killer when it came to acquiring companies through leverage, when his stock was at disproportionately high multiples, but operating a business day to day, especially under difficulties, was not his forte. Because Ray wanted Macmillan to survive, he did what he felt he had to do, tighten the operation. And tighten he did, until it hurt. Orders went out to cut everything, not just to the bone but to the marrow, including the supply of paper clips. Throughout the organization staffs were trimmed, resulting in strikes and strike threats in some divisions. No replacements could be hired or capital purchases made without written approval from headquarters.

What did this mean to Laury? Trouble. He now had to operate with minimum staff. Raises had to be approved by headquarters. He could not replace worn-out equipment or furniture, nor could he even buy a reconditioned typewriter. His expense accounts, and those of his executives and salesmen, were scrutinized. No longer could he travel first class, which he was accustomed to doing, and he could stay only in low-priced hotels or cheap motels. Suites were out. If he wanted his wife along on business trips, as he always did, it would be at his personal expense. His own income was frozen, with no chance of a thaw. In fact, it even looked like he might have it cut. As a result, his pleasant lifestyle began to change. Worse still, he began to lose the excitement of coming to the office Monday mornings. Ditto for other SRDS executives. And, of course, SRDS could no longer expand or dream of doing so. Laury's business as well as his personal life was not what it had been before the now-regretted sale. (And speaking of regret, another mistake he made was to include the new SRDS building in the deal. He could have kept that and remained Macmillan's landlord at an annual rental that could have afforded him additional income, plus some leverage of his own.) For Laury Bothoff, the merger game ended in disaster.

Ian Ballantine is almost a legend in the book publishing business. A highly creative bookman, considered a genius in the special area of paperback publishing, he was a paperback pioneer. For a time he headed the United States branch of Penguin Books, England. He was the first president and publisher of Bantam Books, the largest paperback publisher today. It was he who put the stamp of successful, creative paperback publishing on Bantam. Now headed by Oscar Dystel, Bantam was recently sold, or rather resold, to IFI International, a business conglomerate founded by the famous Agnelli family, for $70 million in cash.

So what happened to Ian? Following a disagreement with his associates, major stockholders, and other board members, Ian left Bantam. With the proceeds from the sale of his stock and additional capital from friends and willing investors, he launched his own paperback business in the late fifties under the imprint of Ballantine Books. His wife, Betty, was his principal associate and working partner. Knowing his way around the publishing club—and book publishing is a private and exclusive club in many respects—Ian prospered from the start. The only thing that restrained him from making Ballantine another Bantam was capital, a very important element in book publishing. It takes a year or two, sometimes longer, for a successful book to return its invested capital, not to mention profit. Not all books are profitable, and usually the publisher still has to pay an advance on future royalties to the author. Often the sum is high. The publisher also assumes all costs for type, printing, and paper, and even must carry his wholesalers and retailers. Not until a book is sold to the reader does the publisher realize any income.

Thus, while Ballantine Books was doing exceedingly well and bringing out some exciting titles (as publishing jargon goes), its growth was stymied for lack of capital. The answer? Merge. This way Ballantine would get money for growth, and Ian would be able to concentrate his talents on creating and developing books.

Inasmuch as the Ballantine operation was still fairly new, only marginally profitable, and not particularly leveraged, Ian had to settle for the best mate he could find. In 1969 Ballantine Books merged into Intext, Inc., a small public company traded over the counter, whose original business was the old, well-known International Correspondence School. To this, Intext's management had already added several other companies, mostly in printing, binding, and book publishing. Since Ballantine was Intext's first paperback house and since paperback publishing was exploding, it seemed an unusually good fit. Ballantine's stockholders received 80,000 Intext shares which, at the merger, were selling at $38 each. Of the total $3,040,000 realized, Ian and his wife received 50,000 shares valued at $1.9 million. Not bad, Ian thought. Moreover, he would now have access to the capital he needed to build his business, which continued as a division of Intext with him as its head.

Great? Definitely not.

In less than a year, Intext stock, which had been selling at unrealistically high multiples, began to plummet, bottoming at $4 a share by 1970. The stock held by Ballantine's shareholders was restricted and now amounted to the sum of $320,000. Ian's share was just $200,000. If he sold (that is, if he could find a market even at $4 a share), and after paying capital gains tax, his total take would be $120,000 to $130,000—not much for practically a lifetime of work and distinctly a beating for the former president and substantial stockholder of Bantam Books.

But this was not the worst of it. Intext's capital structure and credit situation were such that it could not provide Ballantine the capital he needed, not only to expand but even to operate. As a result, Ballantine as an Intext division began to show losses and Ian as a human being became depressed as he tried to exit from his box. Soon, with corporate losses mounting to dangerous levels, Intext decided to sell some of its properties. Despite its own losses, Ballantine Books was easily one of Intext's best.

Thus, Intext financial executives went to work and developed a prospectus for the sale of Ballantine Books. The price tag? Believe it or not, $14 million, based largely on built-up five-year projections. Copies of the prospectus with a covering letter were mailed to selected book publishing chief executives, presumably hot prospects for the property. Several showed interest and negotiations were under way within a few months. The most serious bidder turned out to be Random House, which was in a good position to utilize Ballantine's potential.

In the meantime, Ian, who had been experiencing a great deal of frustration and anxiety, including sleepless nights and dread of losing everything, followed the good advice given by his wife and friends and took a firm stand. He would not approve any deal for the sale of Ballantine Books, and most certainly not unless he got a piece of the action. Because Intext was anxious to sell and Random House willing to buy, Ballantine Books went to Random House for $6 million, not $14 million. Ian did indeed receive a piece of the action with his Intext stock, but only several hundred thousand dollars.

That was in 1973. Ian remained with the new Random House division for about a year, helping to put it in working order and developing several important, well-selling titles. In 1974, once again, he decided to go it alone. He became what is known in the book trade as a "packager," a publisher who creates books selectively and publishes them on a contract basis. Since a packager does not have a distributor setup of his own, he uses the services of an established publisher. Bantam Books is currently distributing Ian's books issued under the imprint of Peacock Press Books.

Ian went through a great deal of personal and financial hell from the time he sold his business to Intext until it was spun off to Random House, and for a good part of those years he looked much older than a man in his early fifties. But at least this merger story did not end entirely on a sad note. It could have been a lot worse.

When Warren Buffett was at the University of Nebraska, from which he was graduated after only three years, he discovered *The Intelligent Investor*, a book by Benjamin Graham. It gave him the key to investment success. By his middle forties he was a multimillionaire and chief executive officer of a widely diversified business with annual sales of a billion dollars—all the result of sophisticated acquisitions. Now 46, Warren is still largely unknown in the business world generally, and in investment circles in particular, basically because he is a private person with a low profile philosophy and policy. But this may well change, attributable mainly to a front-page feature given Mr. Buffett in the March 31, 1977, issue of *The Wall Street Journal*. How he reached his present heights, with plans for even bigger things ahead built on the merger and acquisition game, is both original and fascinating.

After Nebraska and at age 20, he matriculated in the Graduate School of Business of Columbia University where his favorite author, Mr. Graham, taught finance. Teacher and student became friends. In 1954, after a short stint as stockbroker in Omaha, Warren returned to New York and joined the Graham-Newman Corp., an investment fund Mr. Graham headed.

This association and the experience it gave him was Warren's first step on the road to a personal fortune and a billion-dollar conglomerate. In 1956, Warren left

Graham-Newman and with his wife Susan, whom he had married in Omaha four years earlier, returned to his favorite city.

Shortly after setting up their Omaha residence, Warren launched his own business, an investment trust partnership, with three friends and four relatives. Everyone got along nicely, and Warren began to practice what he learned from Mr. Graham's book, his courses at Columbia, and from his experience with Graham-Newman.

Mr. Graham had developed a defensive, statistical approach to stock investment, based on a company's intrinsic value. Simply stated, his theory is that the price a private owner would be willing to pay for a business, based on its net worth, largely its cash and other current assets after deducting all liabilities, represents intrinsic value. Following this approach, Warren Buffett began to buy undervalued stock for the trust partnership, which by then included almost a hundred limited partners, plus the original ones.

Warren Buffett's signal success was his purchase of a substantial block of American Express Company stock, at a time when it had declined sharply as a result of the company's involvement in the famous edible oil scandal. Tanks that were supposed to be full of edible vegetable oil were found to be empty, and American Express took a multimillion-dollar loss. Warren, however, felt the stock was greatly undervalued. He sensed that the company could make a quick recovery. American Express was developing a dominant share of the travel and entertainment credit card business, while its traveler's check volume had not declined. Within two years, American Express tripled in value and Warren sold his bundle for a $20 million gain. He made other stock investments and trades like that during the go-go sixties. Thus, in a little more than a dozen years, Warren Buffett, operating quietly from Omaha, did what a lot of so-called smart Wall Street investors failed to do—he converted a $100,000 partnership investment trust into $100 million. Then in 1969, using another skill—his keen sense of timing—he liquidated the fund and distributed the gains among his hundred partners, just before a sharp decline in stock prices.

With his share of the profits, a cool $25 million but not by other standards a particularly huge sum, Warren Buffett began to build his billion-dollar conglomerate, not in the sixties, but in the early and mid-seventies when so many high-flying conglomerates began to fall apart.

Interesting too, in buying the companies for his conglomerate Warren Buffett followed the principles that helped earn his first $25 million. He bought undervalued companies (or big blocks of their stock) and used only as much leverage (borrowings and credit) as he considered "safe."

This actually began in the mid-sixties when his partnership group acquired control of Berkshire Hathaway, Inc. The once famous New England shirtmaker and producer of other textile products had apparently lost its position in the marketplace, largely the result of declining Maine textile operations generally, and its stock was below liquidation value. Following his basic defensive buying principle, Warren bought. Now, as chairman and chief executive officer with 53 percent of its stock, Warren has BH on the track to profitability and new growth. He did it by using its excess cash (instead of loans and other forms of credit) to diversify into equally profitable, growing fields, such as casualty and automobile insurance, and banking when he acquired the Illinois National Bank & Trust Co., Rockford, Illinois, one of the more profitable and successful regional institutions. Berkshire Hathaway's net earnings, meanwhile, rose to $16 million in 1976 on sales of approximately $140 million, a remarkable achievement.

Warren Buffett looks forward to the rest of the seventies and early eighties with control of, or a substantial minority investment in, a variety of other industries, ranging from a highly regarded regional candy company to newspapers. He owns more than 60 percent of California's Blue Chip Stamps, which in 1976 earned more than $11 million or 12 percent on sales of only $88 million, unique for a business of this type. Because stamp trading went into decline several years ago, Blue Chip moved to acquire more promising businesses. Blue Chip now owns See's Candy Shops, a prestigious and highly profitable Far West candy manufacturing and retailing operation, and 80 percent of Wesco Financial Corp., Pasadena, a savings and loan association. The *Buffalo Evening News*, Buffett's entry into newspapers, was acquired by Blue Chip for $33 a share. He did this as a diversion from money management, but also because newspaper work, with its social and political implications, excited him. Thus he also has substantial investment interests in other newspapers, including the *Boston Globe* (through his holdings in Affiliated Publications, Inc.). And through Affiliated he has interests in Ogilvy, Benson & Mather of London and The Interpublic Group of Companies, Inc., two large advertising agencies. Warren is particularly excited about his 10 percent stock ownership of the Washington Post Co., which in turn owns *Newsweek* magazine, the Trenton, New Jersey, *Times*, and five TV and radio stations.

The list is long and growing. For Buffett it involves a lot more than gaining "industrial power." More important is the personal fulfillment and special joy he gets from both accomplishment and his involvement with people in a business environment. This happens to be a feeling I share. It has been my own belief that if an industrialist accumulates businesses and millions or billions just for the sake of money and power, personal happiness and professional fulfillment will not necessarily follow. There have been a great many unhappy and unfulfilled accumulators. But if an executive works, builds, and grows because he desires fulfillment and gets fun out of doing what he's doing, his chances for success can often be limitless.

Now we turn to the SuCrest story—a story of success and failure, both.

SuCrest Corp., a publicly owned sugar and specialty products company, was founded and built and is still controlled by the Taussigs: the late Charles A. Taussig, once an adviser to President Franklin D. Roosevelt; his brother Richard; Charles's widow, Ruth; her nephew, Robert Simons; her son-in-law, Allerton D. Marshall; and Peter Taussig, Richard's son.

SuCrest, with approximately $100 million in annual volume, was an old, highly regarded but sleepy company until about 20 years ago. It peaked in the late fifties but because it had real growth potential a number of suitors attempted to buy it, to no avail. The Taussig family, with working control, embarked on a growth program of its own, through acquisition and product diversification.

In 1960 SuCrest bought three companies, each in a specialized area of the food ingredient industry: American Breddo Co., Lanco Products Co., and Food Products Development Co. American Breddo and Food Products Development manufactured ingredients largely for the baking industry; Lanco produced ice cream ingredients for the dairy industry. When Food Products Development was sold, Bob Rappaport, its vice-president, was 29 years old, bright and ambitious. The company had been launched and nurtured by his father who died shortly before SuCrest acquired it. The three companies were merged into one under the name of Breddo Products Co., and the combined operation was headquartered in Kansas City where Food Products Development had been located. Bob Rappaport was named vice-president and general manager of the new division. Sales of Food Products Development amounted to only $1 million at the time of the merger and combined sales of the three companies were less than $5 million. By the mid-seventies, however, under Bob's direction division sales had increased to approximately $25 million, with profits up substantially. It also had a much enlarged line that included emulsifiers, dough softeners, stabilizers, and flavors.

Since the sale was for stock, Bob, his brother Richard, and their mother now had substantial interests in SuCrest, while SuCrest became increasingly aware of Bob's creative and management talents. Before long, he was promoted to the presidency of the Breddo Division and several years later, elected to SuCrest's board of directors. By 1974 he became president and chief executive officer.

The Sweetener Division, languishing as one of the lesser sugar refining operations, began to grow. It grew substantially after SuCrest acquired Revere Sugar Co., of Boston, in 1974, shortly before sugar prices increased sharply. By 1975 SuCrest's sweetener business showed record sales of $349 million and profits before taxes of $25 million. The company's total sales were $416 million (before taxes and interest expense of $23 million). Even when the price of sugar declined from a high of about 64 cents to less than 25 cents per pound, SuCrest's Sweetener Division performed more than satisfactorily. Sales in 1976 amounted to $225 million with profits before taxes of $3 million (from total sales of $302 million and profit before taxes and interest expense of almost $9 million).

At the same time, interesting growth patterns were developing in the company's other divisions, notably the specialty products group. Under the capable and creative stewardship of President Vincent V. Amato, in his mid-forties and very able, several important new products were developed and marketed, among them some promising ingredients for the pharmaceutical field.

So everything was coming up roses for SuCrest, pushing toward $500 million in profitable annual sales, and for its aggressive, 45-year-old CEO, Bob Rappaport, who had divided SuCrest's structure into four profit centers: the Sweetener Division, the Specialty Products Division, the Breddo Food Products Division, and the Xtravim Division, with a president for each. It proved an excellent move and the divisions grew and prospered.

Then, based on a detailed account in the SuCrest 1976 Report to Stockholders, this is what happened. As a result of an investigation by the Securities and Exchange Commission and an audit by S. D. Leidesdorf & Co., Su Crest's independent auditors, the company disclosed that two raw sugar transactions in 1975 and 1976 were not fully revealed to the corporation's directors. According to SuCrest's 10-K statement (part of its 1976 report), Mr. Rappaport is represented as having spearheaded the transactions. In an arrangement apparently made solely for accounting purposes, SuCrest bought raw sugar from the Philippines before the end of its 1975 and 1976 fiscal years, to ensure there would be no invasion of its last-in/first-out inventory base. (Under LIFO, a common way of handling sugar and other commodity inventories, the cost of goods is based on the most recent prices for raw materials and other types of inventory items, thus reducing the ballooning effect that inflation has or can have on profit.) Following the end of both those fiscal years, certain members of the SuCrest management resold the sugar as part of an oral agreement. This was not disclosed to the board or to the company's independent auditors. Leidesdorf subsequently ruled that the transactions were not sales after all, and insisted that the company revise its figures for both years, which it did. Su Crest's restated earnings for fiscal 1975 dropped to $5.5 million or $3.05 per share from $16.2 million or $8.89 per share. For fiscal 1976, ending May 29, the revised earnings were $2.7 million or $1.51 per share, not the $7 million or $3.84 per share previously announced.

Out of this highly complicated and technical transaction came Bob Rappaport's resignation, ending, on December 16, 1976, what had appeared to be a brilliant, nonstop career, and for the company a future of profitable growth.

A little earlier, however, knowing his resignation was probably imminent and undergoing great personal stress, Bob Rappaport suffered a heart attack in his office in the presence of the Sweetener Division president, Bud Azarow, and his wife, a registered nurse experienced with cardiac arrests. Bob recovered from his heart attack, but it is doubtful he will fully recover from his one apparent mistake. Bob's actions, which resulted in his resignation, were in good faith and involved no personal gain. He thought he was doing the best for the company he headed, but he did not fully advise his board of directors in time and properly. No explanation for this neglect was given, and the strange part of it is that he had a friendly board of directors, just about all of them of his own choosing.

In addition to everything else, it cost SuCrest almost a million dollars in extra accounting and legal fees and incidental items. It also created a lot of negative PR in the industry and on Wall Street.

Following the company's annual stockholders' meeting on March 31, 1977, the acting chief executive officer, Walter E. Dennis, a financial consultant who as a Su Crest board member is chairman of the audit committee that investigated the sugar transactions, said that the company expected the SEC to take some kind of enforcement action, perhaps in the form of a consent decree. (Under this not uncommon procedure, a company neither affirms nor denies that it was involved in a wrongdoing. Rather, it states it will not engage in whatever the activities were.) First, however, the SEC would have to initiate a complaint claiming that SuCrest violated the law, for any such agreement to be considered. Although Milton N. Scofield, the company's general counsel, confirmed that his discussions with the SEC have revolved around a consent decree, he said the company would fight any claims of wrongdoing in court. Also, while Mr. Rappaport was the only officer forced to resign, Mr. Dennis said after the stockholders' meeting that other members of SuCrest's Sweetener Division were also aware of the transactions. He did not say whether any current director, officer, or employee took part in the decision to make the transactions without informing the directors or accountants of it. He also hesitated to say whether any member of the SuCrest board or management team who might have been aware of the transactions thought they were wrong; but during the stockholders' meeting, Mr. Dennis vigorously defended the audit committee's investigation. "There was no dishonesty and no self-interest in any of these transactions," he said, adding that SuCrest had nevertheless taken steps to strengthen internal controls in the wake of their disclosure.

Meanwhile SuCrest, now headed by Rudy Eberstadt (who left the presidency of Microdot, Inc., following its acquisition by Northwest Industries, Inc.) as president and CEO, announced that it was disposing of its sweetener business, representing two-thirds of its total business, to a privately held company. The proceeds were to be used to accelerate the development of its more profitable, growing, and innovative specialty product divisions, whose total annual sales are approximately $75 million, in hope of taking the firm back to where it was in 1950.

The story of Henry G. Parks, Jr., is unusual in another way. Mr. Parks is black and the founder of H. G. Parks, Inc., a meat products company famous in the Northeast and Southeast for its advertising: "More Parks Sausages, Ma. Please?"

Mr. Parks, Atlanta born and Ohio educated (he was graduated from the College of Commerce of Ohio State

University), started his business career in 1942 as a national sales representative for the Pabst Brewing Co., a rare position for a black at that time. He was most successful. Two years later he left Pabst. With another black, former Pabst salesman W. B. Graham, he founded a public relations and advertising agency under the name of W. B. Graham & Associates, headquartered in New York. The company did fairly well but not well enough. In 1948 Mr. Parks left Graham, still only a two-person agency, and moved to Baltimore at the coaxing of William L. Adams, a mover and doer in the business as well as the politics of Baltimore's black community.

The reason he took Mr. Adams's advice was that Mr. Parks dreamed of starting a business of his own, producing Southern types of foods. And as it developed, Mr. Adams helped Mr. Parks make the dream real. He became Mr. Parks's "silent partner" when he launched his sausage business in 1951 with a bank loan (very difficult to obtain then) and two employees, housed in an abandoned dairy. Mr. Parks created the formula for the sausage and did his own selling. He and his two helpers produced enough sausage in one day to meet sales demand the next. Success came slowly, and as it did Mr. Parks was able to negotiate another loan, and then renew both, one to build his present plant. From here things improved substantially. As a matter of fact, Mr. Parks did so well that in 1969 he took the company public.

In time, however, Henry Parks realized that he had a decision to make. He was approaching 60, a critical age in his opinion, and although Parks sausages were selling well and the company was making money, it was not growing fast enough to satisfy him. The plant was nearly at capacity and he knew he would soon need more capital to expand it and his marketing, and thereby to grow internally. Or he could sell or merge Parks and grow that way.

After pondering these alternatives and consulting his silent partner Bill Adams, he decided that merger would be best. He held exploratory talks with more than a dozen suitors and in the end married his company to the Norin Corp., another OTC company also in Baltimore, doing business largely in life, fire, and casualty insurance, real estate, motels, and recreation. Parks was Norin's entry into the food business.

For his 158,000 shares, Henry Parks received $1.58 million, which even after capital gains taxes made him at least a minor millionaire. (Adams received the same amount for his own 158,000 shares.) With 1976 sales of $14.7 million and net earnings of just over $480,000, $10 a share was not a bad deal, for buyer or seller. It represented better than ten times 1976 after-tax earnings. (The balance of Parks's shares, held publicly, was acquired by tender.) Besides this, Mr. Parks negotiated a satisfactory seven-year contract to remain as chairman of H. G. Parks, a division of the newly formed Norin Food Products, Inc., a wholly owned subsidiary of Norin Corp. What he relinquished, however, was the business he founded. Raymond S. Haysbert, also black and Mr. Parks's former first assistant, has taken over as chief executive officer of the Parks business—the business it took Parks a quarter of a century to build, plus many more years of dreaming.

Let's look now at Lester Rosskam, president and chief executive of the Quaker City Chocolate & Confectionery Co. Inc., Philadelphia. Rosskam represents the fourth generation in this highly regarded, medium-size, profitable candy company famous for its Good & Plenty brand. Approaching 50, in good health, with a nice family and satisfactory lifestyle, he liked what he was doing and was reasonably successful, but in January 1974 he sold to the American Chicle Division of the large pharmaceutical firm, Warner-Lambert Co.

When I met him later that month at a Chicago trade meeting, Lester was all smiles. "Did you take stock?" I asked. "What's that?" he replied. Stock even of Warner-Lambert, a very solid company, was not for Lester, a bit of a maverick in the industry with a special philosophy and approach to business. Although he did not reveal the cash amount he received, it is reputed to have been $3.7 million. Because the sellers in a cash deal normally pay capital gains tax, the net amount would be approximately $2.4 million. This, or whatever it was, he shared with his brother and other family members.

I asked Lester why he sold his business. His quick answer: "Estate problems." Then I asked what for me is the key question: "Do you think you will be happy working for a huge public company?"

He smiled his most charming smile and said, "Absolutely. I will continue to be president and chief executive officer of Quaker City and I will be running the business just the way I have been doing these many years. After all, we are operating a successful, profitable company, so why should there be any changes?"

I could have told him, but there seemed no point in dampening his enthusiasm. Privately I gave him one year in his new situation. The average business life of a chief executive officer who sells out to a public company and continues as division president or general manager is between two and three years. I felt that an executive with Lester's strong independent personality could not last more than a year in a corporate structure like Warner-Lambert's.

Early in 1975 Lester called and gave me the big news: He was resigning his post and leaving Warner-Lambert. When I met him several months later, he said he was planning to write a sequel to my book, *Divorce Corporate Style,* but would call it *Corporate Rape.* Lester, a man of a few select words, proceeded to say that he disagreed with everything that Warner-Lambert wanted to do with Quaker City. In return, Warner-Lambert seemed to disagree with Lester's own modus operandi of running the business. All this, despite the fact he was assured during earlier negotiations that he would continue as "boss man" of Quaker City, meaning he could continue operating it his way. "And all that endless, stupid reporting. . . ."

It should be mentioned that Warner-Lambert is an excellent company, well managed and headed by an able chief executive. I have known Burke Giblin personally more than 25 years, from the time he was president of the Walter Baker Chocolate Division of General Foods, to

54

his stint as a GF executive vice-president, and after that as president of Warner-Lambert. Not only is Burke a brilliant corporate executive, he is also a fine, warm, considerate human being. Nevertheless he is a no-nonsense CEO, and he has surrounded himself with a group of young, capable people who manage the affairs of each division in the modern manner. This does mean plenty of reporting, professional supervision, and interaction with all of the corporation's subsidiaries and divisions. *C'est la vie* in today's corporate world. But for a man like Lester Rosskam, or for that matter any independent, irascible entrepreneur, it's hardly *la vie en rose*.

What happened to Lester? He joined forces with Robert Oram, retired general manager of M&M/Mars, to form Rosskam-Oram, Inc., a management and marketing consulting company. Lester was to handle operations in the East, while Bob, who lived in Chicago and Palm Springs, would direct the business elsewhere, especially in the Far West. But even this arrangement did not last. Within a year the partnership broke up, although in a friendly way and despite the fact business was reportedly brisk. Lester is now on his own. Ditto for Bob. It just goes to show how an independent entrepreneur like Lester Rosskam, with his own strong ideas about how things should be done, may be unable to accommodate himself even to the needs of a two-person partnership.

Still, there are always exceptions. A good one is Robert Kinney. In 1940, Bob was a high school history teacher in Carmel, Maine. During one summer vacation, while traveling through the lobster-fishing areas of his state, an idea occurred to him. Maine lobstermen, he learned, normally threw away crabs that got trapped in their lobster pots. Since crabs are a tasty and valuable food product, he discussed with several lobstermen the possibility of buying (and then reselling) their discards. The lobstermen were delighted by the prospect of extra revenue, and soon Bob exchanged teaching for crab canning. He took to the business world easily and did exceedingly well. With his eye on accelerated growth, he hired a manager for his crab canning operation and in 1953 joined Gorton's Fisheries of Gloucester, Massachusetts. At that time, Gorton's annual volume was less than $8 million, but Bob Kinney had an idea how to make it bigger. Management liked what it heard and invited Bob to take action. He succeeded from the beginning, and as he continued, Bob moved up the corporate ladder—and quickly.

Within four years he was president and chief executive officer of Gorton's. By 1968, a particularly hot merger year, Gorton's sales had reached $74 million. With bids flowing in from various sources, Kinney sold the company to General Mills, Inc. It was a good move, a perfect fit. In the first place, because Gorton was growing rapidly it needed increasing capital to grow more. A point was reached when such capital was obtained only at prohibitive cost. For General Mills, Gorton's was an interesting growth company, well managed, and in Bob Kinney it saw a talent that could be used in its own corporate hierarchy.

So what happened? By the mid-seventies, Gorton's

sales were twice what they were in 1968 and profits had increased substantially. Bob Kinney has indeed moved up the ladder. In January 1977 he was named chairman and chief executive officer of General Mills, almost a $2.5 billion public corporation, to succeed the hugely able Chairman James P. McFarland.

Why did Bob Kinney make it when so many others failed? Among his long list of qualities are tact and patience. Said Bob in a recent interview: "When I see something that I believe needs to be done, I find a way to get attention without having the boat get completely swamped. I don't like to spend all my time bilging water."

That may be a lesson for us all—but a lesson few of us learn.

Chapter

2

View from the Buyer

PETER GRACE, PRESIDENT and chief executive officer of the multibillion-dollar W. R. Grace & Co., fiftieth on the *Fortune* 500, has been involved in many mergers and acquisitions during the past ten years. Expounding his view of the game he said, "A corporation substitutes formal planning for the business intuition and sometimes instinctive planning of the entrepreneur in an effort to improve on the utilization of available resources; but this process is not a substitute for the gifted individual, whose initiative continues to be encouraged and expected within the broad limits set by the corporation."

True enough and well meaning, but it does not always work out that way. W. R. Grace is a good case in point. Originally a shipping and banking company founded by Peter's grandfather 120 years ago, its business mix has changed drastically, especially since the 1950s. It was Peter Grace, a creative, compulsive worker, who initiated and directed the changes. Long ago he foresaw problems, some insurmountable, in the shipping business, especially the kind Grace had been actively operating in South and Central America and in other restless parts of the world. He also realized that his banking business lacked a base big enough to deal with coming difficult situations. His decision: get out of shipping and banking and into chemicals. It looked like a dangerous gamble to some people, including his family and stockholders, when Grace bought two fairly unimportant chemical operations, and in doing so entered into competition with the giants. Nevertheless, it turned out to be a correct, judicious business decision. Today Grace derives its $3.5 billion volume mostly from chemicals, such as industrial and specialty products, packaging and plastic chemicals, fertilizer and other agricultural chemicals.

W. R. Grace has done exceedingly well, mostly through acquisition, but has had its share of failures and frustrations, primarily in the consumer products areas, despite the fact Peter Grace is a cautious buyer. Before a proposed acquisition goes before the board of directors, a great mass of information is gathered scientifically. Teams of experts interview key executives of the company under consideration, study its operation from every possible angle, and then test their data against a highly sophisticated set of Grace standards and measurements. Only after months of this type of study and analysis is the acquisition team ready to say yes or no to the deal. If yes, it goes to a management team for further study and from there to the board of directors.

Still, Grace has failed with a number of acquisitions which on its numerous planning charts looked like winners. When an acquired company does not produce profits or meet Grace's growth patterns, it is quickly spun off, sold, or dropped—in most cases sold off and frequently at a capital gain. There is little dillydallying with an unsatisfactory acquisition. In 1974 alone it sold four packaged foods businesses in the United States. Nalley's Fine Foods, a successful regional snack and specialty operation, was disposed of in 1975 for $15 million. Leaf Confectionery, U.S.A. also went. The price, cash and notes, was less than $5 million, even though in 1967 Grace had paid $14 million in Grace stock. Also disposed of was the famous retail toy operation, F. A. O. Schwarz, which it had acquired in a package deal from George Hecht's Parents' Magazine Co.

How do you explain this in a company like Grace, so analytic, thorough, and scientific? The answer can be found in Grace's phrase *"expected* within the *broad limits* set by the corporation."

Through personal observation and discussions with presidents and managers of companies Grace acquired and later sold, I discovered that it was a matter of how Grace defined such "expectations" and "broad limits" and how he put them in effect. Once again it was people, the interaction of Grace management with the independent entrepreneurs, who spelled success or failure. Peter Grace makes every attempt to hire able executives, but even a man of his ability can make mistakes. Eventually, they are corrected. The executive who looked like a winner, but who wasn't, is separated. The damage has been done, however, and the company must be sold. In some cases, entrepreneurs of acquired companies who may have run their own businesses capably become intractable as managers within a larger public corporation, and thus fail.

Why did Grace fail with Nally's, Leaf, and Schwarz while it succeeded handsomely with other companies it acquired for the same Consumer Division, Herman's World of Sporting Goods and Baker & Taylor?

There is no pat answer. The fact is that each of the companies that failed, failed for a different reason. Each acquisition that proved successful succeeded for a different reason. Still, the answer may lie in the weakness as well as the strength of the Consumer Division itself. Grace today is a chemical business; it is in this area that it placed both the money and talent. Since it was corporate policy to grow and expand in chemicals, this made sense, but it meant allocating secondary talents and less capital to the Consumer Division. Consciously or otherwise, compared with the Chemical Division the Consumer Division became a second-class operation.

Leaf is an example. A major candy and chewing gum company headquartered in Chicago, Leaf was acquired as the "flagship" operation of what was to be for Grace a growing and highly profitable candy manufacturing and marketing business, international in scope. Several years earlier Grace bought the Ambrosia Chocolate Co. of Milwaukee and the Hooton Chocolate Co. of Newark, which it soon placed under one management.

THE NEW MERGER GAME

Ambrosia/Hooton manufactured a number of chocolate products, which it sold to candy manufacturers and other users. It was through this operation that the Consumer Division became interested in the candy business. Leaf, a substantial user of chocolate, became Grace's first candy acquisition.

Negotiations were also conducted with several other candy firms. At one time, Grace came close to acquiring the Fanny Farmer Candy Co., but called the deal off because it feared FTC or SEC disapproval, and possibly other difficulties with the government in acquiring different food concerns. Instead, Grace bought Wayne Candies, Inc., of Indianapolis, a family-owned regional bar goods firm, and the Pearson Candy Co., Los Angeles, also a regional and family concern. Both were fairly small but successful and profitable. Both had substantial growth potential, especially Pearson, whose Coffee Nips had begun to be marketed nationally with spectacular success. With good intentions but limited planning, Wayne and Pearson were placed under the Leaf banner. The result was a string of serious management mistakes, which, compounding over time, eventually jeopardized both the profitability and growth of the whole candy operation.

The initial mistake was to hire a food executive and place him in charge of the division's newly formed grocery products unit, whose total volume exceeded a half-billion dollars. Grocery products soon became a miniconglomerate itself and all product lines directly or indirectly in the area of food, including candy, chocolate, seafood, and snacks of all types, went under its supervision. Drastic changes in management, personnel, administration, and marketing were made throughout the grocery products unit, quickly and without consulting the operating heads. This failure to communicate with unit chief executives, some of whom had been presidents of acquired companies and knew their businesses as only entrepreneurs could, resulted in resentment and a damaging job insecurity. It was not long before the operating units began to fall apart. Instead of being asked the reasons for the newly developed problems, able and experienced group managers were put on the shelf or dismissed without explanation.

By the time the executive vice-president in charge of the Consumer Products Division realized what was happening in grocery products, it was too late to save the operation. Most of the units were spun off, a few to their first owners and at lower-than-acquired prices. Interviewed shortly after the debacle, the former chief executive of one major acquired company that was spun off by Grace made the following comment:

"Basically, the aborted Consumer Products Division failed because of people failure—failure to properly communicate with and utilize the available pool of experienced management talent."

He went on to explain that shortly after he was "detached" from his position as divisional chief executive, he phoned Peter Grace to tell him with displeasure what happened to his division, and to the grocery products unit generally. Sufficiently friendly with the chief officer, he did not hesitate to say what he thought the scenario would be for the months ahead. He told Mr. Grace that he foresaw a dismantling of grocery products six months after its chief executive would depart for more important, higher-paid jobs at an equally large, prestigious corporation. That is exactly what happened.

The failure of the grocery unit was basically a people failure, but it was also the failure of Grace management to realize soon enough what was going on. It took them almost a year to recognize that the executive hired to head grocery products was not only failing to expand the unit and increase its profitability, but knowingly or otherwise was actually inhibiting it.

Why? He had creditable credentials. He had spent the better part of his business career in the food manufacturing and marketing business, reaching the post of executive vice-president of one of the country's largest, most prestigious food corporations. Even so there was sufficient evidence that he had "people problems." For psychological or other reasons never fully explained, he tended to be dogmatic and abrasive. He was apparently not a good listener. Often he infuriated managers under him because he failed to accept, or even listen to, suggestions of a constructive nature, or at least suggestions the managers believed were constructive. As a result, instead of motivating managers to "do better," he tended to frustrate them and their efforts to function effectively. So eventually he was separated from Grace, but by then grocery products was in disarray. Sell-offs and spin-offs took place.

We note the "people problem" again and again in merger situations. What happened with Grace grocery products is merely one example. Entirely too often, outsiders are brought in to manage or direct acquired operations; just as often, failure results. Outsiders seem unable to motivate, understand, and work with entrepreneurial managers like Dan Pearson and Sam Shankam, successful executives who built their own businesses with talents that could have been utilized effectively by the new parent company.

This diagnosis seems correct, because a year after the spin-offs the new owners of Grace units reported gains in market share, sales, and earnings of their acquisitions. At Leaf, the new owners were a group of its original managers. Immediately upon reacquisition, they regrouped product lines, introduced new items, tightened up management, and followed strict budgetary controls. The result was new trade excitement and success in the marketplace. Much the same happened at Pearson, the candy business Grace sold to the Planters/Curtis Division of Standard Brands. In less than two years sales more than doubled, a loss was turned into a substantial profit, and a growth program was well beyond the planning stage.

The Grace grocery products experience offers a few management truisms of the merger and acquisition game:

1. Products alone, no matter how good and accepted they may be, will not guarantee the success of an acquisition. You also need good people—highly motivated

executive talent that is encouraged and given the opportunity to manage and develop.

2. An acquisition may be a disaster for one buyer but an enviable success for another. The outcome depends on what is done with an acquired company and how it is positioned in the marketplace.

3. A highly skilled manager may fail in one particular slot but succeed in another. Also, some corporate managers can leave one major assignment in which they have failed and obtain an even more important job with another company. This type of executive sees the handwriting on the wall and usually departs before the failure can be blamed on him.

4. Determining what to do with an acquired company requires a great deal of thought and planning, which should always include tactful coordination with the incoming management. Careful supervision is then important, especially at the start of the marriage.

5. If an acquisition goes sour, a quick spin-off, usually by sale, is normally best.

6. A corporation may fail with one acquisition but succeed with another. It depends on the circumstances, timing, and the position of the acquired company and its products and services in the marketplace.

Grace succeeded with Herman's and Baker & Taylor, but failed with F. A. O. Schwarz and others, for a number of interesting reasons.

Timing was crucial to their success with Herman's, a small but aggressive and expanding sporting goods retail store company. Long before Grace acquired it, Herman's management knew what was happening in its marketplace. It saw that the field would eventually explode, not only with new varieties of equipment but also wearing apparel, especially as tennis and skiing became the "in" participative sports. This it conveyed to Grace management. With acquisition and new capital, Herman's grew from a few stores in one marketing area to the largest of its type with several hundred stores, some of them department stores, and a much larger market. Quickly it went national. Grace supported this type of program, an important source of its own sharply increased sales and profits. Good management, effective corporate direction, and excellent capital utilization combined to make Herman's one of Grace's most successful acquisitions, as well as the star of the otherwise clouded Consumer Products Division. That it operated entirely apart from grocery products, reporting directly to the Consumer Products executive vice-president, also helped.

Baker & Taylor was successful for another reason. When acquired, it was already by far the nation's largest book distributor. It also had good management, headed by a financially oriented president who came with the deal from Parents' Magazine Co., where as a division it was the most profitable. What B&T needed was the muscle of more capital, some worthwhile acquisitions, and management backup. This was communicated to Grace, and Grace management provided it. Baker & Taylor soon was a sophisticated computerized book distributor, with essential strategic warehousing facilities and a management team backed up by know-how in acquisition exploration.

It took H. J. Heinz Co., Pittsburgh, 103 years to achieve $1 billion in annual sales. H. J. Heinz launched the company in 1869 with one product, horseradish, which he sold door to door to neighboring housewives. New products were introduced, the company grew, and eventually it boasted its famous "57 varieties." Today it manufactures hundreds of products, marketing them in 150 countries and territories, and is well on its way to its second billion in sales.

This came about internally and through acquisition, although that did not really start until 1963, when Heinz bought Star-Kist Foods, Inc. Best known perhaps for its canned tuna, Star-Kist also had other highly regarded foods that blended with Heinz's condiments, catsup, canned baked beans, baby food, and frozen pizza pie.

In the seventies, however, Heinz decided to enter the industrial product field, focusing on corn processing, and to do it by acquisition. What Heinz management liked about corn processing was its growth potential and the new opportunities it saw developing in high fructose syrup. Compared with regular corn syrup, the high fructose product has a far bigger market. It was the first and only product that could compete directly with sucrose, sugar refined from cane and beets. High fructose was already capturing a sizable share of the sucrose market in soft drinks and other beverages, and research showed that its total potential market was almost unlimited. Just about every important corn processor, and at least two sugar refiners, embarked on high fructose development projects. One constructive economic result expected from the high fructose boom is a lessened dependence on foreign sugar supplies. Corn is plentiful in America.

So Heinz moved in. Fewer than a dozen companies processed corn syrup, corn starch, dextrose, and other corn products, and just about all were divisions of large public corporations. This limited the selection. The only potential partner was the Hubinger Co., of Keokuk, Iowa, the smallest corn processing firm around.

Heinz began to romance Hubinger's management early in the seventies. Its attentions became ardent in 1973, when sugar prices at record highs ranged from 60 to 70 cents per pound. With sales until then below $40 million, Hubinger had been only moderately profitable (1972 sales, $40 million; net profit after taxes, $309,654 or 33 cents per share). For several years it even reported losses. Its OTC stock was depressed to $10 a share, from nearly $30. However, with the advent of high sugar prices, the pace of high fructose development accelerated. Soon it replaced cane and beet sugar in a long list of products, at lower cost, and industrial sugar users turned to it in droves. The fortunes of just about all corn processors, including Hubinger, started to improve dramatically. By 1974, Hubinger's sales were $86 million, with net profits after taxes of 5.3 million, or $5.86 per share, compared with 1973 sales of $57 million and net profits after taxes of $2.2 million, $2.40 per share. Its stock had advanced to $15 a share, whereupon Heinz made a "firm" offer of $25 a share.

Even though Hubinger's board of directors said it would not recommend selling at that price, negotiations began. And, by the time Heinz acquired it in 1976, the price was more than $60 a share—about $42.1 million in Heinz stock. Simultaneously, sugar prices declined sharply, and with them went corn products prices, including the price of fructose syrup. The latter was in the area of 15 cents a pound, with sugar futures quoted at less than 10 cents a pound. In 1976 Heinz had committed more than $30 million to take Hubinger into the high fructose syrup business, with its new facility scheduled to go on stream in 1978, as other corn processors moved to postpone construction of new, or more, high fructose syrup plants.

On the surface, and certainly in the shorter view, the Hubinger acquisition seemed an overpriced mistake. From the long-range viewpoint the investment may pay off. In buying Hubinger, Heinz acquired valuable technology and management in the corn processing field, and particularly in high fructose, which in time will surely be *the* alternate to cane and beet sugar. Still, this does illustrate the vast importance of timing in merger/ acquisition situations. It was superbly profitable timing for Hubinger, but was it poor for Heinz? Time will tell.

Of the 25 largest *Fortune* 500 companies, International Telephone and Telegraph Corp., eleventh, has an annual volume of almost $12 billion. Unique in many ways, ITT grew to its present heights almost entirely through acquisition, although its record of internal growth is also impressive. ITT's acquisition program has been so aggressive, in fact, that it has caused certain problems. After buying the huge, cash-rich, billion-dollar-plus Hartford Insurance Co., the nation's fourth largest, it entered into a consent decree with the Justice Department (1971) by which it agreed to divest itself of several other important companies acquired during the previous decade. Among them: ITT Canteen Corp., Grinnell Corp., Avis, Inc., and Levitt & Sons.

As of December 31, 1975, Canteen was gone and control of Grinnell, 61 percent of Avis, and Levitt had been transferred to an independent trustee pending disposal. Avis, "No. 2" in the auto renting business, was sold in mid-1977 by the trustee to Norton Simon Inc. at $22 a share. Of the total shares, 3.7 million represented a spin-off from ITT. The balance, 4.2 million, was held by the public and in mid-1976 traded on the New York Stock Exchange for as low as $9 a share. Canteen, the food and vending company, went to TWA and became the airline's most profitable operation.

ITT had not been too unhappy to lose these firms, except for Avis, but it can hardly wait to get rid of Levitt, once the nation's largest real estate and home construction company. ITT has already lost more than the price it paid in 1968—$92 million in ITT stock. ITT was selling then at $62 a share, or 24 times earnings. In mid-1977 ITT common was at $32, eight times earnings. As of the end of December 1975, however, ITT's net investment in Levitt amounted to approximately $150 million.

The fault in ITT's failure with Levitt seems to be more with the parent company than with William J. Levitt, former chairman and chief executive officer. Successfully involved in other business ventures, with plans to return to his first love, real estate and home building, he remains one of ITT's largest stockholders, although the value of his stock is less than half what it was when he sold his company to ITT. Why did ITT fail, while before the merger Levitt had been a spectacular success? There are many reasons, some complicated, others not so complicated. Among them was the failure of Levitt's original management—especially Richard M. Wasserman, Levitt-trained and Bill's alter ego, who took over—to adjust to the reporting, direction, and general impenetrability of ITT's corporate structure, as it oversees acquired companies. Dick soon departed in disgust, and with him went a score of other key executives. Another basic reason for ITT's failure was, ironically, the capital beneficence it bestowed on its new subsidiary. It appears the money was used unwisely, drawing the Levitt organization into unknown, unexplored, and obviously unproved housing experiments, such as clustered houses and mobile homes, all a far cry from Levitt's original business, building single-family units.

With its numerous subsidiaries, divisions, departments, and compartments, and with more than 400,000 employees, hundreds upon hundreds of executives including a slew of executive vice-presidents and 35 vice-presidents, ITT is clearly not a one-man business by strict definition. Nevertheless, it is fully the creation and the image of one man. Harold Sydney Geneen. Bill Levitt, in an insightful report in *Business Week*, described him as "a computer, a fantastic brain." He added, however, that "he is not perfect and his management system did not lend itself to [Levitt's] business. Geneen and his management team tried to control this company the way they controlled Continental Baking [one of ITT's earlier acquisitions and the nation's largest baking firm]. In [home building] you have got to be able to turn on a dime. Besides, we are a bunch of rugged individualists." Obviously, ITT has no room for rugged individualists except one—its chairman and chief executive, Harold Geneen.

It is hard to believe that a 19-year-old advertising space salesman for the old *New York World-Telegram*, who earned less than $50 a week in the Depression, moved up to head one of the nation's 11 largest corporations. Hal Geneen now earns one of the biggest salaries—more than $800,000 per year—of the country's half-dozen highest-paid chief executives. Almost 300 divisional and subsidiary managers report to him and he runs a tight ship with an iron hand. Practically no vital corporate decision is made without Hal Geneen having his say. Moving around quickly, traveling with several attache cases filled with facts, figures, memos, and notes, on the telephone almost constantly, he is in touch with everything that involves corporate business, asking the right questions and giving the right answers.

For the moment, his avalanche of mergers is at an end, although some selective acquisitions still are made.

Geneen's aim is to add a billion dollars in sales each year, or 10 to 12 percent, through internal growth of the corporation's ten basic companies, rather than by putting out millions of shares of stock for new acquisitions. (It took about 80 million shares to buy the companies ITT owns today.) The real question is what will happen to ITT minus Hal Geneen. To the surprise of a lot of people, Mr. Geneen selected Executive Vice-President Lynon C. Hamilton, Jr., 50, to be CEO following his retirement, scheduled for the end of 1977. In the meantime, Mr. Hamilton will serve as president and chief operating officer. Geneen has also separated his operating executives from the board of directors, largely "friendly" outsiders, all very carefully chosen by him. Of seventeen directors only seven are ITT executives, five of whom are Hal's closest associates. In this way Hal Geneen has full control of the board, which includes investment bankers, business consultants, bank officers, and heads of other corporations, most of whom he had known for a long time, some intimately.

What is life like on the job for a subsidiary president or division manager in Hal Geneen's outfit? Practically a year-long battle to make, or improve, his budgeted bottom line. How is the budget arrived at? In a series of stages beginning in February and March when one- and five-year projections or "objectives" are presented, later reviewed. Meetings come next, at which presidents or general managers defend their estimates and plans. More reviews follow. When programs are finally accepted, further adjustments are made—upward or, if necessary, downward. (Fine tuning seems the rule rather than the exception.) Usually in the fall, final budgets are forwarded to the subsidiary and division presidents, or general managers, and these they must live by. Final budgets are sacrosanct. Operational chief executives have learned, some the hard way, to make sure that their initial projections and estimates are neither too low nor too high, but realistic. Otherwise, stiff questions and warnings come fast.

Even when budgets are accepted and finalized, operational managers are constantly supervised and watched (oh, ever so carefully). If problems are sighted in a division, a team of experts is dispatched quickly to make needed recommendations or take necessary action. And all the while, planning is under way for next year's round. Life for the ITT operational managers may be tougher and more scientific than for those in other diversified public companies, but the idea and format are the same. Projections, planning meetings, jockeying—finally the budget, the gospel, is accepted and approved. The manager had better make his bottom line or have a damn good explanation. If he senses danger, he had best call it to the attention of his direct supervisor rather than have him discover it himself, since the supervisor certainly will, sooner or later. Almost constantly the operational manager is under headquarters' surveillance. If he makes budget or improves on it, he is a hero. If he does not (unless he has solid reasons) he is a chump. The pressure is severe.

Many are the reasons for merger failures. Poor

agement, a weak market position, hiring an inexperi-
ed manager or group after the original entrepreneur
leaves are some. Losing interest in the operation, which
happens more often than people realize, is another; slow
adjustment to market changes, still another. But one of
the most frustrating reasons is "bad fit." An acquired
company can lead its field, but if its type of business is
basically out of kilter with the goals of the parent company, it is destined to fail.

An example of this type of failure is found in the
acquisition of Random House, Inc., by the RCA Corporation. A prestigious and successful book publishing
house owing much of its market charisma to one of its
founders, the late, famous Bennett Cerf, Random House
was acquired by RCA in 1966. At $40 million it was
recognized as a good, solid buy. Mr. Cerf and Robert
Sarnoff, then RCA's chief executive officer, were
friends. Each respected and admired the other. To Mr.
Cerf, Random House chairman and chief executive
officer, "publishing and electronics are natural partners
for the incredible expansion immediately ahead for every
phase of education." To Mr. Sarnoff, the "knowledge
industry," the blending of the then-new computer
technology with the more seasoned business of information in print, seemed a good fit. Besides, at that time Wall
Street favored mergers of this type—high-technology
computer operations melded with print media. Additionally, Mr. Sarnoff liked the image such an association
would provide him personally, and would give RCA in
the market and on Wall Street.

But that is not the way it worked out. RCA's entry into the knowledge industry was, from a business standpoint, disastrous. Book publishing and electronics proved to be unnatural partners: they did not blend. Moreover, RCA failed in the high-flying computer game. Early in the seventies it abandoned its huge computer investment and took a $200 million-plus write-off. By 1976, RCA had decided to sell Random House, despite the fact it continued to publish successfully, because success in book publishing differs considerably from success in electronics. Book profit margins and profit growth are low, very low for some firms, compared with what they are in electronics, RCA's basic business. A 5 percent annual growth is considered good in book publishing. Profit margins are rarely better than that and are often worse. Electronics, on the other hand, has averaged from 10 to 20 percent in growth. Similar profit margins are not unusual and are higher in some instances.

Besides these developments during the ten years after the Random House acquisition, Cerf died and RCA Chairman Bobby Sarnoff retired. The corporation's new CEO, Edgar H. Griffiths, following other executive changes, programmed RCA to improve its profitability. Low-margin Random House had to go. Thus, early in 1977, negotiations were in progress to sell the entire book publishing company, which included Knopf and several other well-known, highly regarded book subsidiaries, to The Times Mirror Company of Los Angeles. The price was less than the $40 million RCA had paid. It appeared to be a bargain and a fine fit. Times Mirror owns and publishes the successful *Los Angeles Times*, as well as other newspapers. It also has a book publisher, but smaller and without the trade acceptance Random House and its satellites have. After several months of negotiations, however, the deal fell through. RCA still wants to sell, but whether it will be able to depends on finding a "desirable" buyer willing to pay RCA's rock-bottom price.

Can a book publishing company fit an electronics operation? Yes and no. Whether a merger like this will work rests with the companies themselves, their goals, marketing approaches, and most important, with the people situation. Had Bobby Sarnoff continued as chief executive officer and had Bennett Cerf lived, this could have been a good merger, even though under such circumstances book and electronics companies may not have been integrated. Electronic and print media do have much in common. Experience reveals they can blend, or at least exist side by side in the same family. Capital Cities Communications, Inc., one of the more successful and fast-growing companies in electronic media, has done exceptionally well with Fairchild Publications, Inc., publishers of *Women's Wear Daily* and other business magazines. In the ten years since Capital Cities acquired Fairchild, its publication or print division has started its own, and acquired other, publishing properties, including daily newspapers like the big, successful *Kansas City Star*. Capital Cities paid more than $125 million for the *Star* and believes it a bargain. It might be. And CBS, the nation's largest electronic media corporation, after a not too auspicious start, is now doing well with its print media acquisitions. It owns W. B. Saunders Co., one of the more important and profitable medical text publishers; Holt, Rinehart & Winston, general and other books; Popular Library, paperbacks; and a strong list of special interest consumer periodicals. Its latest $50 million acquisition: Fawcett Publications, Inc., publisher of books and consumer magazines, including *Woman's Day*. There is also McGraw-Hill, Inc. From its start in business magazines, it moved into books and various services. It recently acquired a chain of TV stations and is doing well with them, and plans further expansion of its electronic media operation. There have in fact been many more successes than failures in electronic/print media combinations.

The merger of Microdot, Inc., of Greenwich, Connecticut, with Ben Heineman's Northwest Industries, Inc., Chicago, had just about all of the elements of a successful corporate marriage. Although far from a total failure, it is not fully successful.

To understand what went wrong, let us examine some details. In 1975, the General Cable Corp., a neighbor of Microdot in Greenwich and a long-established manufacturer of wire and cable, made an "unfriendly" takeover bid, offering $17 a share at a time when Microdot's stock was selling on the New York Stock Exchange at $11.75. Although some stockholders may have considered this offer interesting, the president, chief executive, and founder of Microdot, Rudolph Eberstadt, Jr., wanted no part of it. Then 50 years old, he had other ideas about how to expand his specialized fastener manufacturing company. Besides, he was not impressed with General Cable's record.

The problem Rudy Eberstadt faced was little different from those facing many chief executives of medium-size, even large, corporations that grow mainly through acquisition. He and his close associates lacked the shares to ensure "working," if not total, control of their operation. This is the penalty paid by many managements of expanding, acquisitive public corporations. Their own stock becomes dangerously diluted, following a series of mergers and acquisitions, when new common voting stock is issued to make such deals.

Rudy Eberstadt, friendly but hard hitting, took over in 1960 at age 35, when the small Republic Industrial Corp., of New York, was practically unknown. Young Rudy then used Republic as a handle to acquire a fairly large hodgepodge of other companies and in 1968 hooked a big one—Microdot, Inc., a West Coast manufacturer whose fasteners had real growth potential in the field of electrical connectors. Republic Industrial soon became Microdot, Inc. and moved to Greenwich, not far from Rudy's home. By the time General Cable decided to make its unfriendly bid, Microdot's annual sales exceeded $300 million, with net earnings of about $12 million.

Realizing his vulnerability, Eberstadt figured that if the business he had built were to be taken over, it might as well be by a corporate family he felt comfortable with. At any rate, it would be by a partner of his choosing, not

VIEW FROM THE BUYER

a raid. To accomplish it quickly and well, he sought the
help of Goldman, Sachs & Co., the large Wall Street
investment bankers highly sophisticated in mergers and
acquisitions. It was not long before Goldman, Sachs
found the marriage partner Rudy wanted—Ben Heineman's Northwest Industries, Inc.

Ben is a star of the merger game, prominent in
Chicago's banking and social circles, and has an enviable
record of successful conglomerating. With annual volume nearing $2 billion, Northwest's business ranges
from sophisticated technology, wearing apparel, steel,
fluorescent lamp ballasts, pesticide chemicals, to French
wine and brand-name liquor (such as Cutty Sark scotch).
Ben started it all with a railroad shell, a well-developed
acquisition program, plenty of imagination, and good
financial acumen and backing. In less than ten years, he
built Northwest into an operation of almost 2 billion
annual sales, with almost $120 million in net profits after
taxes, almost entirely through mergers and acquisitions.
Besides that, or because of it, Ben Heineman understands how traumatic it is for an entrepreneurial chief
executive when the company he built is merged. Thus,
Ben permits, and often will actively encourage, the head
of an acquired subsidiary to run his own show, but always by Ben's budgetary and supervisory standards.

No wonder everything seemed rosy at the closing
when Microdot merged into Northwest in early 1976. By
June 30, 1977, however, Rudy Eberstadt was no longer
president of the Microdot subsidiary. Why, and what
lessons does this teach us?

81

Some of Mr. Eberstadt's reasons for leaving were "little annoyances." Others, more subtle, were attributable to matters of dignity, pride, and fulfillment.

"Nothing has changed, and yet everything is changed," Rudy Eberstadt said. "After years of dealing with my own board of directors—people who knew me, trusted and enjoyed working with me, I found myself suddenly confronted with having to account to Northwest for all kinds of little details."

Little or big, subsidiary capital outlays had to be approved by headquarters. A Microdot project involving an investment of $10,000 or more required Northwest's OK, along with all the details—how, why, and what for. It could make no acquisitions itself without Chicago's permission. This meant that Rudy Eberstadt no longer could move as he wanted, quickly and in his own style. Everything had to be cleared. He felt he was no longer his own man. His normal decision-making functions were now subject to approval.

Mr. Heineman, however, said he made every effort to put Mr. Eberstadt and his associates at ease in their new corporate home. "Believe me, I understand that it is difficult for someone like Rudy Eberstadt not to be his own boss." Thus Rudy and his people reported directly to him "so that there would be no personal denigration."

"We know that we have to be sensitive to personalities if we want strong, independent executives running our divisions instead of mere office boys," Mr. Heineman explained. Like other well-run corporations active in the new acquisitions game, he wanted Northwest's subsidiaries and divisions as decentralized as possible, with their presidents having a fair degree of operational freedom.

But for Rudy Eberstadt it was still insufficient for a truly happy corporate marriage. Several of his Microdot executives felt the same. Michael Becker, Microdot's 39-year-old controller who worked closely with Eberstadt, found the merger particularly distasteful. It was his habit to prepare a brief summary of the company's annual budget for profit center heads and top management. Under Northwest's budgetary requirements he had to compile 125 or more pages of the same "summary," so that "they can feed the material in their computer." This he considered an exercise of questionable value. He also found himself "so busy scrambling for Northwest that I do not have time to take care of Rudy Eberstadt's needs." Among Mike Becker's other complaints: "While Northwest focuses on the broad issues, which is fine, some of its executives tend to overlook more specific but important items. For example, they may ask why the fastener group is doing better one month than another but they do not seem to care about any changes at a particular company within the group. Unfortunately, at Northwest we are just a piece of a larger whole."

Allen Howell, Microdot vice-president of corporate development, a job which had involved him in Microdot's own mergers and acquisitions, said that before he could move much more quickly on these transactions. Afterward, needing approval for every such step and because of the excessively long time it took, he became frustrated.

Rudy Eberstadt, Mike Becker, and Allan Howell touched on another disadvantage in working for a subsidiary—the lack of ego satisfaction. Rudy missed following the daily stock transactions of Microdot. Allan, pleased to be promoted from financial assistant to the new post of VP, corporate development, still felt "it would have been nicer to be a vice-president of independent Microdot." All are disappointed that they get no direct recognition for improved sales and earnings. Said Eberstadt: "Because Microdot is no longer a public corporation, when we achieve record earnings [as Microdot did in 1976 as a subsidiary of Northwest] the only place we can go for recognition is Northwest." Before the end of 1977, Rudy Eberstadt took on a new challenge. He became president of SuCrest Corp., in transition, with a gift of stock, options for more, a good salary, considerable incentives—and a new opportunity to be boss man.

What happened to Rudy Eberstadt and his frustrated associates in the postmerger period is not unique. On the other hand, up-and-coming middle managers not only find the adjustment easier to take but actually welcome it as a change. For them, more often than not new growth opportunities can and will develop. The professional manager, especially with an MBA, has very little difficulty adjusting to the new, bigger framework and its demands.

If an independent, strong founder or chief executive of a privately owned company merges it with a large public corporation, he might as well accept the realities. He may continue to head his subsidiary or division but he cannot expect to run the total operation. If he adjusts to the new game plan and moves up in the parent hierarchy, fine. He might even reach the top. It can happen— although that's speculative. What is certain, however, is that he can and should fully discuss his immediate post-merger position, function, and authority, then make sure it is part of his new employment contract.

Of course, the best corporate parent is one with a strict policy of maximum decentralization. Some large public outfits (of which there are not many) buy only established, profitable companies, then expect their able managements to operate on almost a totally decentralized basis, with the authority to introduce new products and make acquisitions. Naturally there is headquarters supervision, but it is limited. So long as sales and the bottom line improve and budgets are met, the subsidiary executive can run his own show. If his record over time proves exceptional, he will surely be elevated in the corporate hierarchy and given greater responsibilities, a larger share of the corporation's empire to handle.

Easily one of the most successful companies in growth through mergers and acquisitions is the American Home Products Corp., New York. With 1976 sales of $2.636 billion and net income of $278 million, American Home shows what can be accomplished by good management of sound, well-integrated acquisitions that .blend into the overall corporate picture.

American Home is a leader in pharmaceuticals, par-

ticularly prescription drugs; in over-the-counter proprietary medicines; and in the specialized food business,
housewares, and kitchen products. Headed by the legendary William F. Laporte, chairman and chief executive
officer, its strength lies in the firm's acquisition program.
From this has come the greatest part of its growth, enabling American Home to increase revenues more than
two and a half times, and net income even better over a
decade. The key is its decentralized approach. Its divisions, practically all acquisitions, operate as practically
separate entities. Altogether American Home has 15.
Just about each has a strong record of internal growth,
the result of capital infusion, creative management, and,
most important, the development of new products and
the expansion of markets.

American Home does not merely acquire a company,
expecting normal growth in sales and profits. It devises
and follows a specific program for each acquisition. It
provides capital and direction for expansion through research and development of new products and through
marketing innovations. If necessary it provides new
management talent or replaces the acquired talent if it
fails to meet corporate goals. These are not shrouded in
mystery. Goals are specific, revealed, strict, and they are
expected to be reached. Dynamic William F. Laporte
gives the management of an acquired firm the after-
tax, net-profit objective of at least 10 percent of sales,
which is not unreasonable. A good pharmaceutical company, for example, with an especially fine record of research and development on new products, can and often

does earn much more than 10 percent of sa
sometimes 20 percent or higher. American Home'
quired pharmaceutical companies include some of
best in the business: Wyeth Laboratories, Ayerst
Laboratories, Ives Laboratories, and Fort Dodge
Laboratories, Ayerst and Wyeth being among the industry's top ten. Hardly a year goes by without each American pharmaceutical division creating one or more new
prescription drugs.

Thus, of American Home's 1976 sales of $2.636 bil-
lion and pretax profits of $544 million, prescription drugs
accounted for 39 percent of sales, 56 percent of pretax
profits. Packaged medicines represented 14 percent of
sales and 16 percent of pretax profits, food products 21
percent and 14 percent. The housewares and household
products division produced 26 percent of sales and 14
percent of pretax profits. Compare this with ten years
ago. In 1967, American Home's sales amounted to just
over $1 billion, net profits after taxes just over $100 million. It will probably wind up 1977 with sales of $3 bil-
lion and net income about $300 million—less than some
of the spectacularly high-flying conglomerates, perhaps,
but built on a more solid base.

There are many reasons why companies buy other
companies. As we have seen, growth is a major reason.
Some look for growth over a long period of time, others
want it fast. Here are cases of each.

James H. Wiborg, president of the relatively unknown but half-billion-dollar Univar Corporation, Seat-
tle, did it the fast way. Also unusual is that he did it with

87

offbeat, financially lackluster, often troubled operations. It all started in 1960 when Mr. Wiborg merged his plastic pipe fabricator with the United Pacific Corp., a financial holding company. With this as a base he went after other companies, his criteria being their potential for a return to profitability and growth. Among these were VWR Scientific, Inc., which distributes laboratory supplies; Penick & Ford, Limited, maker of corn syrup and starches; Treck PhotoGraphic of Canada, Ltd., which wholesales commercial photo products; and The Great Western Malting Co., from the liquidated Columbia Corp.

Treck PhotoGraphic is a good example of the troubled concern Mr. Wiborg has been buying. When bought in 1976, Treck was a loss operation despite annual sales of $90 million. Mr. Wiborg, who paid $12.6 million for it, expects Treck to turn around by 1978. Before this acquisition, Univar's sales amounted to $560 million, with net profits after taxes of just over $14 million. When the new acquisition is fully digested, he expects sales to exceed $650 million, with profits perhaps about $20 million. Elapsed time: two years.

Walter J. Zable, 61 years old, ten years older than Mr. Wiborg, is an entirely different breed. His Cubic Corporation, of San Diego, is a $100 million electronic equipment manufacturer catering to the aerospace industry. Unlike Mr. Wiborg, Mr. Zable built his own business largely through the development of innovative products. In doing so he competed with such giants as McDonnell Douglas, Grumman Aerospace, General

Dynamics, and Singer-Kearfott, and with the biggest of them all, IBM.

Cubic went public in 1959 with a secondary offering a year later. It did not really get into the merger-acquisition game until 1967, however, when it acquired Swan Electronics Corp., a manufacturer of two-way radio equipment. This was followed two years later by the acquisition of the U.S. Elevator Corp., with sales of only $1.5 million. Few paid much attention to U.S. Elevator, but as a result of an infusion of Cubic technology, including the introduction of the industry's first computer-controlled system, U.S. Elevator rose fast. Today it ranks sixth in the business. Other companies acquired by Cubic also enhanced the firm's sales and profits. One was G. S. Parsons Co., a distributor of welding products with sales of only $3 million when Cubic acquired it in 1968. Another was Consolidated Cover Co., with $1.5 million in annual volume. Parsons's sales have increased to $8 million, Consolidated Cover's to $4 million, and now Zable and his associates plan to pick up the pace. As a result, although it has taken 25 years to build Cubic into a $100 million business, management expects to double or perhaps triple the company's volume in the next two or three years.

Chapter

3

The Urge to Merge

IF THE LIFE of a subsidiary president in a large public company can be so dreadful, why should the entrepreneur, the head of a private, family-oriented operation, rush into it? What is this strange, seemingly inexplicable, urge to merge? As one who has observed it firsthand, here are the basic reasons I've discovered:

To a large degree it is psychological. Just about every successful entrepreneur dreams of glory, of identifying with Bigness in Business, with becoming part of a large public company, of sitting on the board of directors, of mixing with corporate royalty. He sees privately owned jets, corporate club life, and the hundreds of other amenities of Big Business. He will rarely admit it but he envies those who have these things.

More pragmatically and most compelling, he wants to take care of his estate. The typical merger candidate is in his fifties or early sixties, maybe his late forties. He has created a business and worked hard to build it. None of his children are interested in the business or know anything about it. His wife may know a little, but not enough to run it. If he dies—or when—what happens to the business, his family, his wife? He has good accountants, expert tax men, and a lawyer he considers his friend, but they don't really understand his business as he does either. Besides, it is still largely a one-man operation. Without him it won't have the same value, but the tax bite could still be huge. With little capital accumulated in the business (since earnings are always plowed back for growth), his family may have to borrow to pay it. Selling his company to a public corporation, however, whose stock is traded actively, will solve the problem. His business will be clearly valued and there will be marketable securities which his family can sell, with the proceeds going to taxes as much as needed. Moreover, there will be no inactive heirs drawing dividends but making no contribution to the company and its growth.

Financial security in the form of marketable stock or a substantial amount of cash serves to settle his worries about his estate. The successful independent entrepreneur usually lives well. He has a nice home in the suburbs, an apartment in the city, or both. He travels for business and for pleasure and usually first class. His children go to the best prep schools and colleges. There is hardly anything of material substance that he and his family cannot have if they want it badly enough. But he has just one complaint. He has very little money in his personal accounts. Just about everything he owns is in the business or related to it in some fashion. He has the strong feeling it would be great to have a big chunk of money, in easily marketable stock or in hard cash, some of which he could invest outside his business, which somehow he feels is always in jeopardy. Get security— it's a strong, compelling reason.

Next is the desire to grow. Mr. Independent Businessman has done well. He has expanded his outfit internally and bought a competitor or two, added a new line through a minor acquisition in another field, but his growth is not great enough. He is restrained by his own limited financial resources and his inability to obtain sufficient venture capital from outside, except by giving away too much of the business. Merging—he never calls it selling—into a large public company seems the logical solution. As a matter of fact, he has had his eye on a very large, important company in his own field, four times as big as his own, which he believes can be acquired, but it would be ridiculous to try. The capital required is beyond his reach. However, if he headed a division of some other large company it could be a cinch. He would then have the marketable securities, cash, or both to pull it off.

And some further reasons: Boredom. After years of struggling to build a private company and not really succeeding, Mr. Independent Businessman becomes bored. He is bored making screws. Running a toy factory. Molding plastics. Manufacturing pantyhose. He feels he has lost the excitement. A merger—never a sale—with an enterprising, fast-moving, diversified public company could renew it, recapture the enchantment of managing and building a business.

Wanting out. Mr. Entrepreneur has had it. He has been working too hard, suffering too many sleepless nights, mainly because he just can't seem to delegate enough responsibility to others, despite the fact he has several able managers, even alter egos. He has found little time, or has just been "too tired," for sports, pleasure travel, hobbies, or to write that novel or memoir, or go back to college for that degree, or maybe even study law. To hell with the business. Sell it, walk away, do what he always dreamed of doing but never had time or energy for.

Illness. He has had one or two coronaries, the last massive, or kidney or liver trouble. His doctor has warned him to take it easy. But how, with the pressure of these last few years? He is worried. He has been brooding about death. Selling the business seems the only answer. His wife has been after him to do just that.

Which brings us to the subject of who should and who should not merge—and under what circumstances.

The independent entrepreneur, who created and built a business in his own style and who enjoyed doing it, should not merge with a large, professionally managed, public company unless he can see the implications fully and accept them. The chances of being able to do this are remote. In very short order, he will awake and become miserable. He will realize he is no longer the owner and chief executive of his business. He is, in fact, an employee of a large corporation, and this will be intolerable. After the awe and excitement wear off, he will discover that headquarters is peering over his shoulder. This will be a pain in the neck, literally. A neurologist may even prescribe a therapeutic collar. Psychologically, the experience will be oppressive and depressing. All those reportings, all those explanations for almost everything he wants to do, major or minor, and which he could do before without *them*—with less effort and so much faster. Those accountants and clerks meandering through his books, lousing up his normal accounting procedures. That goddam spy headquarters installed. He is certainly messing things up, asking stupid questions. And on and on and on. Within a year, two or at most three, this once independent, self-assured personality, now insecure and worried, will pull out in disgust, but he will soon discover a terrible void, a depressing emptiness. Sure he has financial security, but what is its value, its meaning? He has sold—sold, now, not merged—his lifework, his great love, and to such stupid, arrogant SOBs.

Something else could happen too. He could become cautious and fearful. Unable to retire from business itself, he may buy or start a new enterprise. The "noncompete" clause in his merger contract prevents him from entering the same field, or at least not for the next three to seven years. He is not even supposed to take a job with a competing company, although that provision is questionable or subject to interpretation. But who hires a man of 55 or 60? And what do you pay him? Most important, can he work for anybody except himself?

Of course, he could buy or start something in a different field, but after a lifetime in one industry, learning another worries him. He feels insecure, lacking in expertise. Besides, it takes money to start or buy a new business and at his stage of life he fears parting with any significant portion of what he got from the merger. And the longer he waits, the more difficult it is to move; so now he spends more time playing golf, or reading, or he travels more for "pleasure." And broods. With no incentive or excitement, he begins to dry up intellectually and psychologically. He develops all sorts of pains, real and imaginary, and visits his doctor and a list of specialists more frequently. He becomes old and decrepit before his time. Depending on his general stamina, he might even die before his time. It has happened.

Who then *can* benefit from merging or selling? Under what circumstances? As I've made clear, I am not opposed to mergers per se, and in fact I emphasize that there are sound positive reasons for them. Let's look at them now a little more closely.

For the fellow who has had it, but who knows exactly what he will do with his time, selling makes sense. It's a chance to start an entirely new career, or pursue a hobby, with new excitement and plenty of incentive, perhaps even new fulfillment. However, before he attempts the sale at all he should put his house in order. He should do what he can and must to maximize his earnings, to position his company effectively in the marketplace, and to train his key executives so that one of them can function well as the operating head of the soon-to-be subsidiary.

Few well-managed public companies will buy another lacking capable, experienced management.

Selling a second-, third-, or fourth-generation business, encumbered by nonworking family stockholders or "partners," can be an intelligent, practical way of solving a difficult problem, one that could worsen with time and circumstance. The only exception is when the operating head or managing partner is also an independent entrepreneur like the founder, has built the business to even greater heights, and now has a compelling desire to own it. If so he can continue to build and manage the business but still get his nonworking "partners" out of his hair by buying them out through an infusion of venture capital, or better still, through selling off a division.

Merging with a large, well-financed public company can be really valuable when the entrepreneur lacks capital clout but has a specific growth program and a well thought out approach. It is especially advisable for the company president with professional management training or bent who is physically and psychologically healthy and who could adjust fairly easily to the role of a division manager.

But regardless of who the seller is, before getting involved in serious merger negotiations he will do well to examine carefully the buyer's capital structure, past record (say, over the last ten years), its goals and modus operandi. What he should be looking for is the potential for compatibility with his new management—from chief executive down to those with whom he will have the closest working relationship. Another thing is whether the corporation's philosophy will allow him to make substantial investment in the growth situations he had under consideration for his own company. Some won't. This type of corporation usually buys a seasoned, profitable, well-managed company and expects management to build it internally. Thus the method, the approach for planned growth should be thoroughly explored, and before negotiations get serious. This way misunderstandings and future problems can be avoided, or at least minimized.

All this can be crucial in deciding to sell or not to sell, with whom to merge or not to merge. The would-be seller may discover that the way of life in the new corporate hierarchy is not for him, or that it fascinates him. Of course, there is also the danger that he will find himself awed by it. It can be dramatically different from life in his own private operation, and even dangerous. Even more troublesome, lifestyles and operational methodologies change continuously.

But basic principles have not changed and are not likely to. Growth and profitability will continue to dominate the corporate world regardless of the game plans used to achieve them. The able, experienced, creative owner or any chief executive officer of a privately owned business can often adjust to new lifestyles and game plans if he wants to, and if he has fortitude and patience. One who does not have a planned program of growth and lacks clear profit goals won't and can't.

The people element can also be significant in the adjustment process. The head of a privately owned one-man operation will find it almost impossible to adjust to the channels of command of his new parent, where functions are delegated and decisions are made at various levels. But the chairman or president who has been people oriented, and who has developed a capable executive team, will adjust better, regardless of whether his new executive group is made up of gamesmen, jungle fighters, or any other type. The point is, he must learn all he can about the structure of the corporation, its approaches and lifestyles, and must ask questions before he signs on the dotted line.

Sometimes, however, there is a special, extremely compelling reason to merge or sell a company. After building his company from a minor investment into a substantial operation, the entrepreneur suddenly finds himself facing a problem of such financial and psychological magnitude that only by selling or merging his business can he stave off bankruptcy and damage to his psyche. The problem in such situations is the difficulty, if not the impossibility, of finding a merger partner or an acceptable buyer.

Jeff Jaffe started his business career, upon graduating from the Virginia Polytechnic Institute with a degree in architectural engineering, as an assistant in the advertising department of Tootsie Rolls, of Hoboken, New Jersey (now Tootsie Rolls Industries, Inc., Chicago). He was in his early twenties and the year was 1946. Two years later he became advertising manager. But in 1949, his father-in-law, Bert Rubin, who had resurrected Tootsie Rolls from its shambles of the thirties, died of a heart attack. Other members of the Rubin family, who took over at Bert's demise, had different ideas about how to run this special business. Within a few months after these management changes, Jeff left. Still, he liked the candy business and thought it had a future for him. After a year as marketing manager for the old Loft Candy Corp., in Long Island City, New York, Jeff decided to go into business for himself.

Encouraged by his wife, Natalie, Jeff acquired the small, regional Chunky Candy Co. on Delancey Street, the heart of New York's Lower East Side. His initial investment was $25,000. Not much, to be sure, and all it bought was a dormant operation. After some success with a little square bar of chocolate and raisins during the war years when all chocolate was scarce, Chunky's founder, a one-time candy jobber named Phil Silverschein, encountered rough going when the war ended and candy was again in good supply. So Phil decided to call it quits and when Jeff Jaffe came along in 1950, he sold the company for a down payment of $25,000, plus a contingent liability of $60,000. Jeff paid this the following year, and almost immediately Chunky took off. Before long, Jeff moved to a much larger plant in Brooklyn. This enabled him to increase production to the point where Chunky began to enjoy distribution far beyond its original market, the New York Metropolitan area. Chunky, as a product and as a company, continued to grow and prosper.

An able executive, Jeff realized from the beginning that the key to growth in any business is utilizing executive talent well. Thus, he encouraged Al Erlich, his major domo, to assume greater marketing and management responsibility. Al came through with flying colors. (Incidentally, Jeff had hired Al as a very inexperienced young man, when he walked in off Delancey Street and asked for a job—any job. Jeff gave him the opportunity to learn the candy business from the bottom—yes, sweeping the floor and other menial work. Shortly afterward, Jeff brought in Alec Abrahamson, sales manager of Tootsie Rolls, and gave him complete sales responsibility. Alec too came through admirably.)

Well staffed in marketing, sales, and production, Jeff began to devote most of his time to finance and new product development. He went also on the lookout for mergers and acquisitions and soon found his own outfit being wooed. With Chunky running smoothly and growing healthily, Jeff acquired the Schutter Candy Co., an important Chicago bar goods house, boasting one of the industry's most modern plants. Before the end of the same year, Jeff also bought the Klotz Candy Co., fudge maker of Louisville, Kentucky.

Then something unfortunate occurred. Chunky/Schutter was doing $20 million in annual sales when in February 1967 salmonella, that anaerobic bacteria pathogenic to man, was discovered in a batch of chocolate. By order of the Food and Drug Administration, Jeff had to recall millions of candy bars. None was found to be contaminated and there was no record of anyone becoming ill from a Chunky or Schutter bar, but the damage was done. Irreparably. His losses turned out to be so high that the Chunky/Schutter operation verged on bankruptcy, and his once ardent suitors, whose offers had averaged $7 million, cooled off completely. Seven million dollars? No one would take it even as a gift.

But Jeff Jaffe was not one to give up. The one thing he decided *not* to do was file for bankruptcy—even under Chapter XI, which would have given him a chance to reorganize, even though several meetings with his creditors proved unfruitful and presented no tangible way out. Doggedly he pursued a merger-acquisition parent. If earlier his standards had been high, now they were lowered. Almost any offer within reason would be the only practical solution to his terrible financial bind. Eventually he got one from Ward Foods, Inc., headed by Charles Call.

Before going on with Jeff's story, we first have to tell Chuck Call's. It began when Charles Bluhdorn, doing spectacularly well with his Gulf + Western Industries, found himself owning Noma Electric. Once a small but successful electric bulb manufacturer and importer specializing in Christmas tree lighting, by 1962 it was only a corporate shell with $3 million cash in its corporate exchequer. Going to Charles Call, then a financial consultant known for a special gift in doing things with corporate shells and finding implausible merger partners, Charles Bluhdorn said, in effect, take Noma with its $3 million and go find yourself companies to buy. Build a little conglomerate.

And that is precisely what Chuck Call proceeded to do. Early in 1963, he found Ward Baking Co., known for its Tip-Top brand of bread, but financially not too healthy. In a one-sided deal with the Ward management, Chuck merged Ward and Noma and became president and chief executive officer of the combined operation, Ward Foods, Inc., with Charles Bluhdorn a substantial stockholder and board member. From there Chuck Call began buying just about any company in sight whose management was willing to sell. Most of them were not of prime quality, to put it mildly. Enter Jeff Jaffe.

By the time Jeff and his financially struggling Chunky/Schutter came before Chuck Call, Ward Foods, Inc., was a sizable business. Sales were in the neighborhood of $300 million, but its earnings record was unimpressive and it was burdened with huge debts at high interest rates. Still, bad as Ward was, it was the only home Jeff could find, and Chuck Call struck another hard deal, assuming Jeff's debts but paying very little. Jeff did get some stock for his struggling company, however, and most important of all, his contract included a provision for more shares later, based on future results from the Chunky/Schutter operation.

The merger of Chunky/Schutter into Ward took place in July 1967 and everybody seemed happy, including the Chunky/Schutter creditors. They would be paid in full, over a period of years, but from the cash flow and new earnings of Chunky/Schutter, not from the treasury of its parent. Jeff Jaffe, now president of Ward's candy division, began again to restructure his operation and to build it into one of the more successful businesses of its kind, helped by the discovery that the salmonella which

almost ruined him came from a year-old batch of choco-
late coatings supplied by Blumenthal Bros. Chocolate,
Philadelphia. Jeff sued and in 1975 won approximately
$1.5 million in damages from Blumenthal's insurer.
Ward, meanwhile, had acquired Blumenthal through
Jeff's efforts.

This turned out to be an important step in Jeff's
growth pattern. In 1970, his division bought the old,
prestigious Robert A. Johnston Co., manufacturers of
cocoa and chocolate products. A year later he added the
Oh Henry! line of candies. The Ward Candy and Chocolate Division was not only growing but it soon became
Ward's most profitable unit. Thus, in 1972, Jeff was
elected president and chief operating officer of Ward
Foods, Inc., succeeding Chuck Call, who continued as
chairman and CEO.

It was not long before Jeff Jaffe discovered he had
inherited more problems than he had bargained for. He
knew that Ward Foods needed complete restructuring,
but it needed a lot more besides. In attempting to over-
haul, Mr. Jaffe found himself in serious disagreement
with Louis Yaeger, Ward's single largest stockholder.
Since he was unable to obtain the needed cooperation
from Mr. Yaeger and other directors who voted with Mr.
Yaeger, Jeff had no choice except to resign (from the
board, too). He returned to his previous post, president
of the Ward Candy and Chocolate Division. At the same
time, Charles Bluhdorn, who had backed Jeff's position,
also resigned as a director, and eventually both sold their
Ward stock, of which Jaffe held a substantial amount.

After an extensive search, the board of directors of Ward found a new president and chief executive officer, William Howlett, former chairman and chief executive officer of Consolidated Foods Corporation. By now Ward Candy and Chocolate had sales of about $75 million and was clearly one of the most profitable of all the Ward Foods divisions. But after taking a short vacation and giving the matter a great deal of thought, Jeff Jaffe, youthful and vigorous in his early fifties, decided in 1973 to resign the division presidency. He had a future in the candy business, he felt, and had built a "franchise" and reputation for himself. Turning the reins over to Alvin Erlich, he began to seek opportunities.

In 1974 a unique opportunity did, indeed, present itself. Charles Bluhdorn called Jeff and invited him for a chat. Charlie told Jeff that he was offered the Schrafft Candy Co., and asked Jeff what he knew about its present status. He asked him to study this old-line, well-known company, then advise him to buy or not buy it. Charlie told Jeff that if he recommended the Schrafft acquisition, and if Charlie bought it, Jeff would be president and chief executive officer. After a week or so Jeff returned to Bluhdorn with a buy recommendation. Three days later, Gulf + Western Industries went ahead and Jeff took over. That was in July.

Although sales were in the neighborhood of $30 million, Schrafft was losing almost $2 million a year. It was beset with problems accumulated during a long period of inept management under a series of ownerships, the last being Helme Products, the snuff and tobacco company.

Jeff looked at Schrafft as the precise challenge he wanted. He assumed his new post with a great deal of enthusiasm, moved from New York to Boston, hired a new team of managers, and began to restructure the company in his own image. He worked 16 hours a day, 7 days a week, and thrived on it. Injecting new excitement and esprit into Schrafft's employees, Jeff began to see a turnaround almost from the beginning. He changed product lines, created new packages, and effected new marketing and sales approaches. By the end of his first year, Schrafft was able to show a profit. And that, Jeff said, "was only the beginning." He was right. By mid-1976, Schrafft was on solid footing.

But what about Chuck Call? That was a tragedy.

When Charles Bluhdorn invited Charles Call to find a "home" for the Noma Electric shell and its $3 million, in no time at all he found Ward Baking Co., the predecessor of Ward Foods, Inc. Whether Chuck knew or did not know that Ward Baking Co. was seriously on the downgrade was never fully established, but what he actually bought was the Tip-Top name for bread, a listing on the New York Stock Exchange, and not much else. Nevertheless, using Ward as a base, Chuck Call began to build a miniconglomerate—but the kind that resembled a house of cards. To say he was unselective in his purchases is putting it charitably. What he did was to use leverage to get the financing he needed for his highly complicated deals. Chuck was a master with figures and could toss them around in a way that sounded meaningful. The result was a huge debt, with one losing operation after another added to the Ward combine. No operational executive, by the time Chuck resigned as president and chief executive officer of Ward Foods, Inc., in 1972, losing his $140,000 a year salary, he was a beaten and sick man.

Five years earlier, unable to cope with the growing difficulties at Ward Foods, Inc., Chuck, weighing more than 350 pounds with a record of high blood pressure, suffered a stroke which, among other disabilities, left him with no peripheral vision. About a year later he underwent brain surgery but his vision did not improve. He began to suffer depression and by the end of 1974, almost blind, it had worsened. By now he was also doing badly in the investment counseling business he had started after resigning the Ward presidency. Early in the morning of January 2, 1975, according to police reports, the 49-year-old Chuck, who by then looked 65, wandered from bedroom to bedroom in his 15-room house, on 39 acres in Morris Township, New Jersey, and shot to death his 43-year-old wife, Eloise, and their 14-year-old emotionally ill son, Charles, Jr. He then turned the 12-gauge shotgun on himself.

What happened from here on was 180 degrees removed from the Call tragedy. William Howlett and Al Erlich were successful in obtaining the needed cooperation from Mr. Yaeger. Since personal investment was his total commitment and since his Ward stock represented a sizable portion of his portfolio, Mr. Yaeger was now ready to encourage the new Ward management team to take the needed action for a meaningful turnaround.

When William Howlett assumed the direction of Ward in 1972, there were those who thought the corporation's problems were insurmountable. However, before tackling them, Mr. Howlett, soft-spoken with great inner strength and confidence, insisted on two things: complete authority and enough time to do what he felt necessary. That was to move headquarters from New York to Wilmette, Illinois, near his home; bring in a new executive team; quickly sell off the nonfood operations, long a drain on Ward's profitability: and institute more desirable financing.

Unchanged, however, were the candy, chocolate, and dessert group, headed by Al Erlich, and the dairy group, the basic company of which was Marigold Foods, Inc., with David C. Ramsey as president. Not only did Al prove a good administrator and sound businessman, but also a first class, creative marketer. A great help to Jeff and Chunky/Schutter, he was practically a lifesaver for Ward and Bill Howlett. By the end of 1974, Al's division achieved record sales of $89.8 million and earnings before taxes of $6 million. It was this that enabled Ward Foods to report a new profit for the year of $1.2 million, compared with a net loss of $9.7 million in 1973, which had been due in large part to the high cost of interest Ward had to pay for its inherited, excessive debt.

By the end of 1975, Al Erlich's candy, chocolate, and dessert group posted sales of $95 million and pretax profits of $6.3 million, making it one of the largest and most profitable candy and chocolate operations in the country. By this and the excellent results of Marigold Dairies,

THE NEW MERGER GAME

Ward's fortunes continued to improve, creating net profits of $4 million in 1975, despite its continued debt load.

Early in 1976, however, Ward began to experience a new reversal. This was due almost entirely to the failure of the bakery group, Ward's original business and one of the largest in the field, to build on its new profitability in 1975. In his statement to stockholders in the corporation's 1975 annual report, Chairman and CEO William Howlett said:

> The Bakery Group . . . had been neglected in prior years and, therefore, has been slow to respond to the capital improvement program. . . . Additional unanticipated heavy expenses were incurred in completing the consolidation of the New England bakery plants, and in refurbishing the Farm Crest operation in Detroit. The real benefits of these capital improvements are still ahead of us, and should begin to be reflected in our 1976 results.

But this was not to be. Instead of responding to these capital improvements, new problems developed in Ward's bakery group and could not be solved in 1976. Thus, by the end of 1976, the bakery group had a 12-month loss of approximately $12 million. At the same time, the candy, chocolate, and dessert group, under the direction of Alvin Erlich, posted record sales of $99 million and record earnings of approximately $7.2 million. Ward's other profitable divisions showed a combined profit of approximately $7 million, but this was still not enough to overcome its continued high interest costs.

Thus, in January 1977, the board of directors took steps to change the Ward management once again. Alvin

Erlich was elected president and chief executive officer
and given a five-year contract at a salary of $200,000 a
year, plus incentive bonuses, a handsome retirement
program, and stock options. Mr. Howlett remained
chairman but without any specific corporate function,
while Mr. Erlich acted quickly to reorganize Ward's top
management group. Focusing on the unprofitable bakery
division, whose sales of about $150 million were roughly
half the corporation's total, he named Geoffrey Stiles,
vice-president for operations of Ward-Johnston, Inc.,
president. Joseph A. Marshall, Jr., vice-president for industrial marketing, moved up to Ward-Johnston's presidency, and the entire Ward operation relocated from
Wilmette to the general offices of the candy, chocolate,
and dessert group in New York. Before the first quarter
was up and just two months after Erlich became CEO,
Ward was turning around. Sales for the 12 weeks ending
March 19, 1977 amounted to $74 million, compared with
$70.5 million for the same period the year before, and net
income was $1.8 million compared with $282,000—or 47
cents a share against 7 cents a share.

There was no real magic in what he did, Mr. Erlich
said when I talked with him. It was just the result of
good, strong management procedures, which included a
lot of tightening.

But I had other questions.

Why do some executives of merged companies succeed with the acquiring company?

"The biggest single factor is the hard-nosed experience of having had to work for somebody prior to the

merger. It is almost impossible to make it with a merged company if you have been the senior executive for an important period of time. If you have had your own way and your own design for running things and then you are tested for executive responsibility in another milieu, it is really impossible to adjust to the needs of the parent corporation. You are being asked to do something you have never done before in your life. And that is work in tandem and take orders."

Then you must think that it is more difficult for the president of the acquired company to make this kind of adjustment?

"Not necessarily a president. Do not forget that a president may have worked his way up from somewhere and at one time may have taken orders, too. It is the entrepreneurial owner of a business, who created and built his company, who will have the most difficult job to adjust to his new environments and new management needs."

Is there any answer at all for the independent owner in a merger?

"He should be able to operate his own particular division of the merged corporation. He should never go into the headquarters of the corporation in anything except the chief executive officer's job of his subsidiary. With very few exceptions, anything else is wrong. As a rule, he does not have the talent or the understanding of how to give ground. In a lot of situations he is bound to feel he is right, but finds himself unable to direct people to do what has to be done. He must persuade or cajole or compromise to accomplish what needs to be done. That is why it is difficult right from the start."

What is your own business philosophy which made it possible for you to succeed with Ward?

"I happen to be a worker. I like to work and I never did mind working for somebody. I worked for others for a long time. At the same time, I happen to believe that I have always been first among equals. If you want to operate in that kind of environment—the corporate environment—if you allow yourself to think of operating under a hierarchical structure, then you have a chance to succeed with the parent corporation, and may even move up the corporate ladder. It can also be helpful if you follow a philosophy that will permit you to accept challenges to your decision-making functions without fear of being fired or demoted."

Are you saying that you have to be sure of yourself? That you should have a bare minimum of insecurity?

"I follow the basic attitude that I must earn the respect of my colleagues rather than demand it. With a lot of people—especially the entrepreneurial executives, the founders of their own businesses—they have never accepted people coming into their operation as genuine colleagues. They think of them as subordinates. There is no other alternative in the corporate life. Whether you like it or not, if you want to be successful with the corporation that acquired your business there is no other way. You have to convince people to do things. You have got to accept the philosophy that you are a hired hand. No argument on this account. I think most entrepreneurs say, 'I own this company, I built it, and no one is going to tell me. . . .' "

The owner of a business with an urge to merge can learn plenty from the experience of Jeff Jaffe, Chuck Call, William Howlett, and Al Erlich. The variables in a merger situation can be imponderable, complex, and hold many psychological hazards. It takes a strong constitution, a healthy psyche, personal security, and endless patience and perseverance to deal with them and only the exceptional person, endowed with exceptional qualities of leadership, can do it.

Chapter

4

Initiating a Merger

ONCE THE OWNER of a privately held company decides
to merge into a public corporation, at least two basic
problems arise: how to find the most satisfactory partner
and when to initiate the merger.

Although the direct approach is best for the buyer, it
is not best for the seller. Some public companies use
brokers or management consultants to seek merger candidates, and many have corporate development departments whose major function is to identify likely candidates and explore matters with their managements.
However, the direct approach is still used successfully.
The chief executive of a large public company, or his
vice-president for acquisitions, makes direct, personal
contact with the president of the merger candidate, following up with informal, preliminary discussions.

For the seller, however, an intermediary is more
practical and desirable. A direct approach could prove

embarrassing. To some degree, it may be considered a sign of weakness. It would be better to find an ethical, experienced, successful broker, business management group, or consultant with expertise in mergers and acquisitions. But study and research is necessary. There is no shortage of these people, but the number of professional, honorable, and able ones with records of achievement is not large. Also, some brokers and consultants specialize in certain fields, or at least emphasize some industries more than others. Investigation will enable the would-be seller to determine which broker or consultant is best for him.

Often the investment banker is the best possible intermediary. His prestige in the financial community, his acquaintance with a wide range of chief executive officers of the country's more important corporations, his skill and professionalism in handling negotiations and evaluations—all are things to look for, and the better breed has them. You'll find good ones in New York, but also in San Francisco, Chicago, and Boston. Among the best are Goldman Sachs & Co., White, Weld & Co., Lazard Frères & Co., First Boston Corporation, Solomon Brothers, Kuhn Loeb & Co., Lehman Corp., Drexel Burnham Lambert, and Warburg Paribas Becker. Remember, however, that while investment bankers will initiate and manage the acquisition or merger of a small company of $5 million or less, most of the deals involve multimillion- and multibillion-dollar operations.

For these large, growing corporations the investment banking firm performs a variety of services. In most cases it serves as banker, underwriter, and financial adviser, using research capabilities and other valuable resources usually unavailable to the corporation itself or its commercial banker. Most importantly, the good investment banking house is well known in the financial and business community, and in many ways is a special and prestigious club. Thus, when a firm like White, Weld is ready to do an underwriting of, say, $100 million or more (sometimes much more) it has no problem gathering the important participating underwriters it needs (but always by invitation, incidentally).

My own experience was with White, Weld & Co., which completes about 35 to 40 major deals a year, most of them substantial. Most begin with, or certainly include, Paul Hallingby, the personable and astute chairman of the company. One interesting case is the $512 million tender offer made by the $5 billion-plus United Technologies Corp., for the $1.7 billion Babcock & Wilcox Co.

It all started when Mr. Hallingby learned that United's chairman, Harry Gray, had his eye on Combustion Engineering, Inc. Mr. Hallingby felt that Mr. Gray had little chance of buying it, but that he could acquire Babcock & Wilcox in a much better deal. For openers, Hallingby proposed an intensive study, at a cost of about $20,000, to prove his point, and Harry bought it. That was in early January 1977. Paul presented the survey to Harry Gray in less than a month, suggesting that UT make a tender offer for B&W stock at $45 a share when it was selling for $10 less on the New York

Stock Exchange. Although Mr. Gray liked White, Weld's conclusions generally, he thought Paul was out of his mind on the price. Nevertheless, about a month later, at Chairman Gray's invitation, Paul Hallingby presented his proposal to United's board, and by the end of March, UT had made its official offer: $42 a share. Immediately, B&W's stock began to advance. Before the end of June it had passed $45, continuing upward as United Technologies increased its offer to $48 per share, then to $55 against competition from another bidder.

In the end, Harry Gray and United Technologies lost the battle for control of Babcock & Wilcox to J. Ray McDermott & Co., Inc., of New Orleans, a major producer of offshore oil rigs. It was a matter of price and the compatibility of principles. McDermott paid $65 a share for B&W while the most UT would pay was $55 a share. At the same time, George G. Zipf, chairman and president of B&W, preferred to deal with Roy McDermott since he found Harry Gray overbearing. Smith Barney, Harris Upham & Co. served McDermott as investment banker.

All of which provides some insight into the way investment banking firms like White, Weld and Smith Barney, Harris Upham work. A client comes to the firm expressing a desire to buy another company or sell his own, usually with a clear idea of what he wants. At White, Weld (and the other major investment banking houses) he meets with several executives, including the head of the merger and acquisition department, to determine what is available and which is best, then to evolve a strategy. Following that, they settle on a company, amending the overall strategy to fit the needs of a specific deal they hope to make. Meanwhile research is under way. The problem that most concerns White, Weld in a merger and acquisition situation is the fit for seller as well as buyer. Financials of both firms, including the current annual report, the most recent ten-year record, cash flow, product lines, growth potential—all this and more—are studied. When it's over, seller and buyer will have a pretty clear picture of each other. By the time White, Weld makes a specific proposal to the buyer, the seller knows how much his business is worth and to whom. Each will know the other's goals and business philosophy. Most importantly, the seller will know what his own role will be after the sale or merger.

It's clear, therefore, why investment bankers are invaluable. Their research capabilities, their financial, legal, and accounting expertise, and their understanding of the sophisticated psychology of mergers and acquisitions are essential to buyer and seller both. The charge? It's based on cost-plus. It involves the time spent by the firm's key executives, the research required, and the dollar value of the deal itself. Generally it will be higher than what a business broker charges, but in very large deals involving multimillion- or multibillion-dollar acquisitions it can be less. Whatever it is, however, it will usually be just a fraction of the transaction's total value. From my own experience and that of others, it's a small price to pay for so much in return.

It is important to remember that the major investment banking firm selects its clients carefully and hesitates to involve itself with companies relatively unknown to it. Here, a commercial bank could help make an introduction. A chief executive officer of a growing corporation will do well, therefore, to get acquainted early with an investment banking firm, before he really needs its acquisition services. The larger investment banking firms do a lot more than underwrite new issues and set up mergers and acquisitions. With access to large sums of dollars in their role as investment bankers for funds and affluent individuals on the lookout for interesting investment opportunities, they also constitute a prime source for private placements, as well as for seed money for new businesses. Very often they will provide funds to get a company started, then when it is sufficiently profitable take it public, eventually to merge with a larger corporation.

However, before the would-be seller meets with his chosen broker or consultant, he might do well to explore things on his own. A good procedure is to list the public corporations with which he wants to merge. Ask, if I had a choice of a public company to own, what would it be? Remember that the seller will in the end own part of his new parent. How widely is its stock distributed? Does any one family or person own a substantial portion of it? Does any one group or individual have working control? Often the chief executive officer of an important, listed public corporation will own a small fraction, maybe less than one percent, of its stock. This usually means he is a professional manager and may have reached the top through ability and achievement. Which may be good. In

a corporation like this the seller could have real ownership clout. It is not unusual for presidents of privately
held concerns to wind up with more shares than their
new CEO. The seller becomes the corporation's single
biggest stockholder, or one of them, not a bad situation at
all. Jim Weiss, whom we met in the first chapter, owns
more stock in Beatrice Foods than Bill Karnes, the long-
time chief executive officer.

Once the seller has listed his buyers and studied their
records, goals, and principal executives, he is ready to
meet with his broker, merger consultant, or investment
banker. He should now assume the initiative by explaining his objectives and long-range goals, and by describing
the kind of merger he has in mind, the type of company
he wants. All this may sound obvious, but unfortunately,
what is obvious is often overlooked. The broker will ask
questions and here a frank, open exchange can be fruit-
ful. The broker will then want to see the seller's up-to-
date financials and five-year statements—everything the
buyer will want to see. The seller then gives the broker
his list of prospects and after lengthy discussions they
decide which is their first choice, second, third. The
informed and experienced broker will have his own
ideas, which it is wise to listen to. Through this give-
and-take, questions are answered, doubts resolved, and
approaches decided upon.

Finally, before the broker will proceed further, he
asks for (or provides) a tentatively worded agreement
specifying his charges. There are formulas for this but
terms are still negotiable. Of course, before he signs any-

119

thing the seller consults his attorney. This is a must, even if the seller is law oriented, or a law school graduate and a member of the bar. Doctors don't treat themselves, they call in other doctors. Let me emphasize, therefore—don't be your own lawyer.

That done and the agreement signed, the efficient broker wastes little time. The seller will hear from him within weeks, sometimes days. Next comes the first meeting with a potential buyer. Chief executive, president, and chief operating officer, or vice-president in charge of mergers and acquisitions, whoever they are the seller must meet with only the buyer's top people. Usually the broker is there too, but his presence is not necessary. He definitely should *not* be on hand for the later meetings. Private, informal chats between buyer and seller, with no one else around, are vital. Only this way can both parties break the constraints of formality and the psychological barriers between them, essential if such a difficult undertaking as a merger is to succeed. Group meetings will come soon enough, but the early meetings must be private. Nor should the seller bring any paper with him. That, too, comes later. These conferences should be relaxed and totally informal, preferably at lunch. The most that can be expected from the first one is a meeting of minds. Normally, just getting acquainted is sufficient. The seller will also learn whether the interest expressed in his company is serious, exploratory, or merely superficial.

Obviously, after several such meetings, if the buyer is serious he will ask for financial statements, lists and profiles of employees, and a great deal of other information bearing on price and other factors. This stage can go on for months. In dealing with a major public company, such activities can last a year, even longer, before the merger is consummated or ends in failure. Patience, perseverance, and fortitude are tested. Sometimes, during the heat of negotiations, the seller calls them off with such statements as "I do not need this nonsense. It's a waste of time," and walks out on the deal. What he thinks is time-wasting shilly-shallying is actually a necessary routine for the buyer as a way to analyze and evaluate the seller. What may have happened to the seller, in fact, is that he realizes he did not want to sell at all, or he fears what may happen to him and his baby later. If so, he would certainly have been unhappy. Merger with a large, sophisticated, professionally managed public company is not for everyone, even if there are sound, logical business reasons for it. It takes a strong, secure individual to persevere through the negotiations, ceaseless paper work, and endless conferences leading to a successful merger, but it takes the same qualities to succeed in the new company afterward. Owners who do stick it out learn a great deal, however, not only about mergers but about how large public companies operate. Thus, they begin early to adjust to their role as managers in the parent hierarchy. Those who can play the merger game with enjoyment and realistic expectation can have a ball.

During these preliminary negotiations—the "engagement"—the seller is usually treated with respect and deference. He is taken to lunch in exclusive clubs or in private and often luxurious company dining rooms. He is shown the corporation's headquarters, research, and library facilities. It's the full treatment and is pleasant indeed. Without realizing it, however, he may become trapped by his own awe of his intended partners, their surroundings, and facilities, their business lifestyle. The seller must not be taken in; difficult as it is, he must stay objective. What will this mean to me? What price do I pay for it? How will these people behave after the merger? Who are they, really? What are their aims, hopes, and goals? Will I be able to join their world, or must I? Is it really for me? All these he must ask seriously. Or, the seller could be overcome with fear, so strong at times that he becomes unrealistic and antagonistic. This can kill even the best potential merger.

The seller's lawyer or his accountant, especially his lawyer, can also destroy a merger before it is consummated, openly or covertly. This is particularly the case with insecure, not very successful attorneys who consider themselves personal friends of the seller. My job is to protect my friend, this lawyer reasons, but in doing so he puts all kinds of unreasonable questions to the buyer's executives and attorneys—some utterly irrelevant and time wasting, others intimidating. He'll insist on stipulations in the contract that make no business sense. Instead of protecting his client from being taken over, what he really wants, consciously or unconsciously, is to bring negotiations to a halt. This is one reason why the seller should suggest to his attorney that he bring in a law firm that specializes in mergers and acquisitions. Not only can this save the seller time and money, it can assure him of getting objectivity and professionalism.

The same holds for the seller's accountant. If it's a one-person office with no special skill in the intricacies of these procedures, all the more so. The owner of the privately held company must also utilize his own accounting staff, especially his chief accounting officer, almost from the outset, but they must keep such merger discussions completely confidential. Normally, it may be more prudent, therefore, to involve accounting personnel later, when negotiations have matured a bit.

The list of pitfalls facing the seller in a merger situation is practically endless, and all must be anticipated. Based on my experience, I suggest this list of things to watch for:

The owner's stock takes a sudden drop. What do you do?

The buyer's stock advances—dramatically.

Your sales and profits decline during negotiations.

The merger game plan is changed when a new man enters.

Unforeseen changes occur in the marketplace for your principal product.

As negotiations proceed, there are signs that a recession is beginning.

Inflation heats up.

An impasse develops between lawyers.

Problems of evaluation arise.

There are no answers to these questions, nor any surefire solutions to these problems. Each requires special consideration and treatment, but it may help to look at their implications.

What do you do, what does happen, when the buyer's stock takes a sudden drop?

Assuming it's not attributable to a softened market generally but to the company's own activities, try to determine why. Is it because of some bad news, a story unfavorable to the company in a financial publication? An expected decline in earnings? Normally the company will give you meaningful, reasonable answers. If the drop is temporary and explainable, you can wait it out and see what happens, before signing a binding contract.

But there may be more important reasons. It sometimes happens that after an analysis of the buyer's financial statements has been completed, the business will be valued in dollars. If the seller accepts this dollar valuation, it will be converted in a share equivalent, the number of shares the public company will pay for the business it will acquire. Inasmuch as there is no way to forecast the price of the stock on the day the deal is closed, which may be months after the agreement in principle, provisions are made for possible fluctuations. Both parties agree that the price for the acquired company will approximate the agreed-upon valuation, regardless of where the stock is at the closing. Naturally, no major change up or down is expected under normal market conditions during this intervening period, but it could happen. Thus, it should be provided for in the agreement in principle. Obviously, if the price of the buyer's stock has deteriorated for previously unforeseen but basic reasons attributable to the company itself, the seller can exercise his option to call the deal off without recourse or penalty. Similar procedures apply when the price of the buyer's stock dramatically appreciates.

More serious and difficult is when the seller's sales, and particularly its earnings, decline during the negotiations. Obviously, the best thing to do is to come clean with the buyer. If the reasons are good and especially if the drop is temporary, no major change need be made in the contract now being drafted, assuming the buyer still wants to buy. Depending on the circumstance, it is possible that the buyer will propose a price adjustment. Eventually, the price will depend on how well the negotiations go, but also on how much good faith is evident on both sides.

Occasionally an attempt will be made to change the merger game plan. This happens when a new man, representing the buyer, enters the negotiations—say, a new vice-president in charge of acquisitions. He will have his own ideas on the buyer's merger program and chances are they will be constructive. Not only might they involve the method by which stock, cash, or both will be used, but they might also bear on the company's post-merger structure. If the new game does not take anything of intrinsic value from the seller, let it prevail. What the seller must determine is whether the new game plan is in good faith, is for the benefit of both parties, and is not meant to drastically and adversely change the deal, or ease the buyer out of it.

What happens when changes occur in the seller's

THE NEW MERGER GAME

marketplace? Let's say a slump that could seriously affect sales and profits is beginning to develop, or a price war that would not affect sales but could hurt earnings breaks out. No need to call negotiations off, although often they are. Because the seller knows his market and the buyer has learned it, needed now is a full, open discussion. If the situation is temporary, and if the overall industry has solid, long-range potential, negotiations will contine. Or, if the slump or price war is more serious, buyer and seller may agree to postpone the consummation until a specific future date—in six months or a year, but no longer. Proceedings can resume then, or earlier if market conditions show improvement. Similarly, if signs of a recession appear during negotiations or if inflation heats up, the merger may still be consummated, although at a lower or higher price than was originally discussed.

One difficult problem that often develops during merger negotiations concerns valuation. At a certain point the parties cannot agree upon the value of the seller's company. What has to be done, and done quickly, is to call in a professional evaluator or appraiser. This could be a respected consultant with special knowledge of the seller's company and industry, or a professional organization whose function is to evaluate companies specifically for mergers. The professional evaluator or appraiser is often called in by seller, buyer, or both before a price is set or to evaluate the assets before, during, and after the negotiations. This step becomes particularly important when assets are intangible as well as tangible, and cannot be clearly defined. It is not simply a matter of putting a

126

price on the tangibles and estimating the intangibles. The professional appraiser will evaluate such items as original cost, replacement and reproduction cost, tax basis, patents, franchise agreements, R&D, technical knowledge, standing with an industry, staff knowledge, product line importance, goodwill, and a long list of other items, besides such obvious things as land, buildings, equipment, and book, liquidation, and fair market value.

Some of the larger investment banking companies and underwriters handle evaluations too, but whoever does it, it may take a few weeks and sometimes several months. The cost is normally part of the overall cost of the merger and is added to the price when the acquisition is consummated. If it isn't, the would-be seller and buyer share the bill equally.

If an impasse develops between lawyers—a rare but destructive turn of events—an impartial attorney should be called in. A lawyer with expertise in arbitration and merger and acquisition proceedings who is respected by both groups of lawyers will be able to get things moving again.

Chapter

5

With Whom to Merge –and Not to Merge

PEOPLE AND PRODUCTS make a company. They also determine a good or a bad merger. As I said earlier, it is the mix that counts. One case where the wrong mix of both people and products and services played havoc with acquisitions is Genesco, Inc.

Genesco is the billion-dollar child of hard-working, ambitious, once-independent shoe entrepreneur Maxey Jarman. In the sixties and early seventies, Maxey went on an acquisition binge, buying just about everything he got his hands on. In the mid- and late sixties conditions were especially favorable, with public stock at high multiples and underwriters willing. Thus, Maxey Jarman turned his General Shoe Co. into a hodgepodge conglomerate. He bought other shoe companies; manufacturers of wearing apparel; and numerous apparel retailers, such as S. H. Kress & Co. and Bonwit Teller; well-known regional stores like Roos/Atkins; diversified operations, such as Flagg Bros., Johnston & Murphy Shoe Co., Plymouth Shops, Henri Bendel, Inc., L. Grief & Sons, and Gidding-Jenny.

In the bargain (and too many of Genesco's acquisitions were no bargains at all), Maxey got involved with strong-minded entrepreneurs and managers. They wanted no part of Genesco's own type of expertise, including its high-powered financial controls. Maxey, who began to have difficulty keeping track of what he bought and what his managers were doing, eventually lost control. As a result, his son Frank, who had been Maxey's alter ego (or something), took over the business in an effort to save it, installing himself as chief executive. To control its board he reduced the directors from 22 to 12, removing those he felt were more loyal to Pop than to himself and thus likely to give him trouble. His next move was to fire hundreds of managers, including many of the original owners of the acquired firms, which started a sort of corporate revolution and precipitated threats of law suits. None of this helped executive morale. He also began seeking buyers for some of his father's acquisitions. Not confining himself to a few of his regional fashion chains, he even sought a buyer for the prestigious Bonwit Teller. With 13 stores throughout the country, it began losing heavily, and there were no ready buyers in sight. The price asked was $50 million. Meanwhile, president after president came and went, usually in short order. It was pretty much the same at the other operations.

Frank Jarman made a real try to return the company to profitability, credibility, and growth. For a while it seemed he would succeed. In fiscal 1976, Genesco earned $15.9 million, compared with a 1975 loss of $14.9 million, but some of the corporation's outside directors were not particularly impressed, especially since Frank appeared unable to sustain his gains. In the first fiscal quarter ending October 31, 1976, earnings dropped to $2.2 million, or 11 cents a share, from $5.7 million, or 39 cents a share, the previous year. At the same time, while the industry as a whole was gaining, Genesco's sales declined from $294.5 million to $277.6 million. Neither did some outside board members like it when Frank, even with eventual board approval, gave himself a raise in salary from $105,000 to $285,000 a year.

Before the year's end, the ten-man board had called a special meeting, and after a long and tortuous session the outside directors did what they felt they had to. Frank was fired, and William Blackie, 70, was appointed acting president and CEO. After many months of searching for someone permanent they found John J. Hanigan, 65, retired chairman and CEO of Brunswick Corporation and the man credited with its latest effort for a turn-around.

It just goes to show what can happen when a son, no matter how able, tries to work for a strong-minded father.

While there are many Genescos among big, listed

corporations, an equally large number did well. Not only have they survived the trouble of the mid-seventies, but they are positioned to grow in years ahead. One is Tenneco Inc., of Houston. In the five years through 1974 alone, it expanded from sales of $2.6 billion and net profits of just over $120 million to more than $5 billion and net earnings of almost $300 million.

In contrast with Genesco, Tenneco has a much healthier product mix. Most of its acquired companies are in important growth areas with substantial earning potential. Additionally, Tenneco succeeded in helping several top managers (including presidents) of its acquired companies adjust to its big-time operating situation. Interestingly, while Tenneco is heavily involved in pipeline systems and oil operations, its acquisitions have also been in packaging and in agriculture and land development products, as well as in shipbuilding, farm equipment, and automotive components.

Not unlike other large public corporations with well-defined merger programs, the 33-year-old Tenneco continually evaluates the businesses it acquires, and if some do not fit its mix or goals, they are quickly sold off. In 1977, it was well into the second of a five-year program to reorient its chemical business, which management called a "hodgepodge of downstream products," into a more scientific and technologically based operation in heavy hydrocarbons, a field certainly appropriate for an oil company. On the other hand, Tenneco sold off a half-dozen smaller subsidiaries with a variety of product lines, hoping to use the capital it gained to expand its

Houston polyvinyl chloride plant as much as 60 percent by 1978. The upshot is that for 1977 alone, Tenneco expects capital investments to reach $750 million.

Thus we see two in a range of large, listed public corporations that grew mainly through mergers and acquisitions. One is a failure, the other a success. Between these are hundreds more with similar stories. Two are especially worth attention. Although different in many ways, the two are alike in one respect. Both are headed by unique, brilliant, creative, strong-willed personalities: Gulf + Western Industries, Inc. by Charles G. Bluhdorn, and the Rapid American Corporation by Meshulam Riklis.

Of the two, Mr. Riklis is the more erratic and complicated. A former Hebrew and mathematics teacher, Mr. Riklis came to the United States from Israel in 1947 with just $4,000 in his pocket. He located in Minneapolis, continued to teach, but at the same time he joined the large brokerage firm of Piper, Jaffray and Hopwood as security analyst and customer's man. A strange combination of jobs for some people, but not for young Meshulam. As a Hebrew teacher he had entree to some of Minneapolis's more affluent Jewish families, who soon became his brokerage customers. His commissions were substantial, and before long he was able to parlay his connections and earnings into his own business. Soon after his thirty-eighth birthday, and just 15 years after he arrived from Israel, Mr. Riklis had built a $300 million conglomerate. One year later, his company was facing financial disaster. But by this time (he was 39 then) his

company, Rapid American, was pushing toward $3 billion in annual sales.

Among his diverse operations were the McCrory-McLellan-Green variety chain, Leeds Travelwear luggage, Joseph H. Cohen, and Cross Country Clothes. He also owned Glen Alden Corp., the Oklahoma Tire and Economy auto supply stores, varied operations in textiles and building materials, Playtex undergarments, and Schenley Industries, one of the biggest in liquor—a veritable stew, all but a few bought on their decline. He was, in other words, a bargain hunter.

Occasionally his profits were respectable, but over the years and on balance Rapid American experienced heavy losses. Presidents and managers came and went. Mr. Riklis became a trader—he bought and sold companies at almost the speed that stock traders buy and sell stock. Some firms he resold to their original owners, Cellucraft among them. A growing, exciting, medium-size packaging converting company, with a good profit record before he bought it, Cellucraft began to lose money quickly afterward. Mr. Riklis may have had a genius for creative and unusual acquisition deals, but he had little talent in operations, which may have been the problem. In any case, the Luckman and Levy families soon bought Cellucraft back and then took it public.

During all this and despite a poor record of operating profit, Meshulam Riklis became a wealthy man. By the late sixties he began to make major investments on his own, with his own money, but again in run-down, badly managed companies whose names and traditions, however, were well known and respectable—Cartier, Mark Cross, and Georg Jensen, for example, all part of the Kenton Corporation package. He did so badly that within a few years Kenton filed a petition under Chapter XI of the Bankruptcy Act. Somehow Mr. Riklis was able to spin off and sell the three companies, and somehow his personal holdings were not greatly affected.

Then, toward the end of 1975, Rapid American developed a liquidity crunch. Faced with huge losses and pressure from the banks, what did Chairman Riklis do? He did what other corporate chief executives have done in the same spot—sell off profitable subsidiaries or other valuable assets to stay afloat. Riklis sold Playtex, his most profitable unit, for $210 million to Esmark, Inc., formed from the big meat packaging company, Swift & Company. With this Mr. Riklis began paying off his $250 million bank debt. Although this eased the pressure from the bankers, it did not cure the basic illness—continued losses due largely to poor management.

Mr. Riklis, as we noted, seems to thrive on complicated deals, the more complicated the better, so complicated that not many understand them. For example, in June 1977, Kenton Corporation, 36 percent owned by the Meshulam Riklis family trust, pledged all its stock in its Mark Cross Inc. subsidiary to London Brigade Inc. of New York under a $1 million loan and option agreement to Mark Cross effective March 17, 1977. Participating were Edward and George Wasserberger, the principal executives of both Mark Cross and London Brigade. The Wasserbergers also own a majority of the outstanding capital stock of London Brigade. Payment of the loan, at 8 percent annual interest, is due April 30, 1978. Upon receipt, Mark Cross will distribute the million to Kenton.

But it gets more complicated. Kenton has also offered to acquire Shenandoah Corp., a race track operator and maker of women's sportswear and double knit fabrics (an interesting combination) for $19.7 million in cash. In the original loan agreement, Mark Cross also granted London Brigade an exclusive, irrevocable option to purchase substantially all its assets, including its valuable corporate name, subject to the assumption of its liabilities. The option is exercisable from February 1 through April 30, 1978, at a price of $1.6 million, or half of Mark Cross's pretax earnings during fiscal 1978, and the assumed liabilities. If Mark Cross has a loss, the price is to be reduced by varying amounts to a maximum of $400,000. It's all in Kenton's 10-K report.

The same 10-K also shows that in 1976 Mr. Riklis sold his 402,103 shares (36 percent) of Kenton's outstanding stock to Simona R. Ackerman, Marcia R. Kletter, Ira D. Riklis, Arie Genger, and Arnold Broser, trustees of the Riklis family trust. Mrs. Ackerman, Mrs. Kletter, and Ira Riklis are the children of Meshulam Riklis. Mr. Broser, president of Kenton, is also listed as an attorney and a vice-president and director of M-Y Associates, Inc., an insurance brokerage firm that is a subsidiary of McCrory Corp. retirement-benefit plan—and McCrory is the retailing subsidiary of Rapid American. Lorence A. Silverberg, named president and chief executive of McCrory in June of 1977, owns 109,093 shares, 10 percent of Kenton's outstanding stock. M-Y Associates is an insurance broker for Kenton. Mr. Broser is also a tax consultant to Rapid American and McCrory. Again, it is all in the aforementioned 10-K report, along with other interesting items. Besides Messrs. Broser and Genger, other members of the Kenton board are Irwin Ackerman, husband of Simona; Ira Riklis; and Benjamin Kletter, husband of Marcia. Mr. Ackerman is Kenton's chairman. Mr. Genger is a vice-president and executive assistant to the chairman of Rapid American—who, as we pointed out, is Meshulam Riklis.

Also in that 10-K: The trustees and their spouses own a total of 88,265 shares, 8 percent of the Kenton outstanding stock. It is further revealed that Meshulam Riklis had previously pledged his shares with a bank to secure certain indebtedness of his payable on demand. The 10-K report shows that the amount Mr. Riklis owes the bank substantially exceeds the face amount of the note, and that the trustees purchased the shares, subject to such pledge, with payment of the note conditional upon delivery of the shares to them. Mr. Riklis has agreed to use his best efforts to obtain the release of the shares on, or prior to, the maturity of the note, the 10-K report says. It also points out that if the shares are released by the bank prior to the note's maturity, Mr. Riklis has agreed to immediately deliver them to the trustees.

Now as complicated as this may seem, it is a minor, very minor, Meshulam Riklis transaction. To describe one of his major transactions would take a book and to tell the complete story of Meshulam Riklis's merger and acquisition activities from the beginning would require a dozen books. But one thing is clear. Rapid American Corporation is not the type of firm to sell to or merge with, at least not for the independent entrepreneur who wishes to operate and grow with headquarters.

Charles Bluhdorn is a different breed of cat entirely. Although at times he seems almost as reckless as Riklis in his buying sprees, Mr. Bluhdorn is a true builder of corporate structures. Every purchase is carefully thought out and researched, and the firms Mr. Bluhdorn acquires are solid, with excellent records of growth and profit, or with good potential. Owned by his Gulf +·Western are many diverse but bellwether operations, among them Paramount Pictures Corp., Consolidated Cigar Corp. (Dutch Masters, El Producto, Muriel), Brown Co. (paper and building materials), A.P.S. Inc. (automotive replacement parts), E. W. Bliss Co. (can making machinery), New Jersey Zinc Co. (zinc, pigments, metal), Famous Music Corp., Providence Washington Insurance Co., Eagle Signal Co., and Schrafft, the famous candy maker. G + W is also involved in the production of raw cane sugar in Florida and in citrus products with Florida's Indian River brand.

It is not easy to work for Charles Bluhdorn, but in his own special way he gets presidents and managers of acquired companies to stick with him, and he also succeeds in attracting excellent talent from outside. Like Mr. Riklis, Mr. Bluhdorn came to the United States from abroad; he too started with little capital but with great ability, creativity, and ambition. Gulf + Western stock may zigzag from spectacular highs to equally spectacular lows, but the company is basically sound and well managed. Annual sales exceed $2 billion and net earnings $100 million. In July 1975, when its stock had gone from a low of $23 a share (in 1974) to a high of $42 a share, G + W announced a two-for-one split. No longer on an acquisition rampage, it continues to add companies selectively and to buy into large public corporations for "investment purposes," as well as for takeover potential. Charles Bluhdorn is a fair but tough buyer with little patience for mediocre performance. Feeling his stock was grossly undervalued in 1974, he and G + W bought back almost 1.5 million shares, at less than $20 a share. Now, with more shares to utilize for acquisitions, G + W is waiting for still higher multiples before moving aggressively once more.

Not only such hotshots as Meshulam Riklis but others with more successful, highly profitable, tried-and-true corporations got stuck with poor acquisitions, particularly during the bull merger market of the fifties and sixties.

William Paley of CBS, one of the nation's most successful entrepreneurs, had more than his own share of failures. Early in 1951, CBS acquired Hytron, a radio and TV manufacturing operation in Brooklyn, for stock with an eventual value of a quarter of a billion dollars. He did not realize the company had an overabundant inventory of vacuum tubes at a time when the transistor was coming in. After pouring in $50 million more to "save" Hytron, CBS finally gave up and took a huge capital loss

138

write-off. Yet for little more, and maybe even less, it could have acquired a better-known, more sophisticated operation. Then, in the late sixties, CBS bought the New York Yankees for $13.2 million. Bill should have known that this once great team was then on the skids. Several years later he sold, but for $10 million.

Even the great Xerox Corporation has flubbed. In 1969, it paid almost a billion dollars—yes, a *billion* dollars—for the six-year-old Scientific Data Systems. Then, in July 1975, Xerox announced it was getting out of computers, but it could write off only a fraction of this huge investment ($84 million to be exact). All it had left from this billion-dollar fiasco was some technology, which it may or may not have had any use for later.

Should not Xerox have known better than to invest in an untried company in a volatile business, with so little knowledge of either? Max Palevsky, founder and then SDS head, has his own ideas why. "The Xerox management didn't know how to run a lean business and cut corners when corners must be cut," he said. When he sold, SDS was profitable and growing. He believes that Xerox could have made it with Scientific Data Systems, and made it big, had it been willing to compete with IBM vigorously, as a hard-hitting entrepreneur would have, by learning the business and getting the needed talent. Instead, according to Mr. Palevsky, Xerox behaved bureaucratically. Either it failed or refused to tackle IBM head on.

Why, too, would W. R. Grace & Co., with its awesome research and analysis capability, pay $14 million in stock for Leaf Brands, Inc., when it could have bought a really great candy maker like Peter Paul, Inc. for not that much more? And General Foods Corp., too. It never did explain its failure with the Viviane Woodward Co., cosmetics. General Foods also lost plenty with Burger Chef Systems, Inc., the hamburger chain. It's coming around now but in the meantime it depressed GF's earnings and consequently its stock. Another mistake was with Kohner Bros., a toy company that GF finally sold off in 1974. And while all this was happening, its competitors—Beatrice, Consolidated Foods, Kraft, and the others—forged ahead in growth, sales, and earnings.

The list of unbelievably bad operations bought by smart, listed corporations is huge, but the examples cited here will make two important points, one for the buyer and the other for the seller. The buyer must exercise great selectivity and improve his method of evaluation, both of the company he is buying and its market. For the seller there is a different lesson. Don't sell to a big, listed, public corporation unless you can establish beyond a reasonable doubt that the fit makes sense, that your business will really grow under new leadership, and that you yourself can operate successfully and profitably in your new environment. Unless, of course, you just want to sell your baby and run away from it, in which case it's the buyer's problem, not yours.

For example, does it make sense for a food company to buy into the truck body business? For a fashion house to buy a screw maker? For an oil drilling operation to enter the retail discount store business? Or for a magazine publisher to buy a company that makes lighting fixtures?

Obviously it doesn't, yet exceptions exist and some combinations are pretty wild. What counts, however, is a sound, well-financed corporate structure, and a clearly defined merger and acquisition program backed by a professional, highly skilled team. Its sole job will be to seek out, research, and recommend merger candidates to management, and only a talented, creative executive with proven expertise should head it. Still, the buyer should acquire no company unless its management is first-rate and experienced, and unless it is headed by motivated entrepreneurial executives dedicated to growth. Then, and only then, can almost any kind of company be bought—and succeed.

Take Emhart Corp., Farmington, Connecticut. Dating to 1922, it remained fairly small and confined largely to materials-handling equipment until 1964, when it launched a well-conceived, well-planned program of expansion through acquisitions and mergers. In that year, with less than $50 million in total volume, Emhart merged into the American Hardware Corp., a leader in its field, larger than Emhart but not by much. The combination, soon called the Emhart Corp., moved into high gear, and by 1971 was involved in such fields as hardware, materials-handling machinery, store equipment, and allied lines. Sales were just over $212 million and net profits after taxes approximately $24 million. Four years later, annual sales had soared to $355 million, net earnings to $26 million.

But Emhart had just gotten started. It decided to grow again—and again by merger and acquisition, but in a new way. It went after U.S.M. Corp., a worldwide diversified industrial manufacturer with a heritage in the shoe business, but serving other industries too, such as the automotive, rubber, plastics, construction, and appliances. What was unusual about the move was that U.S.M. was almost twice Emhart's size.

It didn't happen easily, however. While Emhart had had its eye on U.S.M. for some time, the move actually started on September 8, 1975, when Emhart made a tender offer to buy a million shares of U.S.M. common. Next day the U.S.M. management responded by applying to the Massachusetts District Court for an order, under the 1953 and 1969 decrees, enjoining Emhart from the purchase. The same day, Emhart brought suit against U.S.M. in the United States District Court for the District of Connecticut, later transferred to the Massachusetts District Court, alleging, among other things, violations of the federal securities laws and the common law arising out of U.S.M.'s public response to Emhart's tender offer.

U.S.M. counterclaimed by alleging Emhart's violation of the federal antitrust laws. What followed was a battle between lawyers. A preliminary ruling by the Massachusetts District Court, on October 21, 1975, denied Emhart's request for certain preliminary injunctions, but in doing so it said that by statements U.S.M. made in response to Emhart's offer, U.S.M. had violated Sections 14(d) and 14(e) of the Securities Act of 1934.

This, the court said, constituted a violation of the fiduciary duties of the U.S.M. directors and officers who made them. In a previous preliminary ruling, October 14, 1975, the same court had issued a preliminary order enjoining Emhart from acquiring or attempting to acquire any securities of U.S.M. pursuant to the tender offer, and from violating or causing U.S.M. to violate the antitrust laws of 1953 and the 1969 decrees. This Emhart appealed to the United States Court of Appeals for the First District. On November 5, 1975, the appeal court entered an order vacating and dissolving the entire preliminary injunction, whereupon Emhart's tender offer proceeded.

By now, however, Emhart's bid to acquire U.S.M. actually appeared "friendly." Takeover efforts by others in the meantime seemed even less desirable to U.S.M.'s management and stockholders than Emhart's. Legal actions stopped and merger transactions started. They did not take long. Papers were signed on May 3, 1976 joining Emhart and U.S.M. into a holding company, New Emhart.

Make no mistake, however. Emhart acquired U.S.M., not the other way around, and took operating control of both companies. New Emhart's board consists of eight original Emhart board members, and only three representing U.S.M., since Emhart shareholders wound up owning 67 percent of the combined U.S.M./Emhart stock. Emhart and U.S.M. divisions are now operated as subsidiaries of the New Emhart team. The bottom line? For the year ending December 1, 1976, total sales were more than $1 billion; net profit approached $44 million. A year earlier the old Emhart's sales were $355 million, net earnings $22.6 million. A nice start indeed.

Another thing. No professionally trained manager can operate and manage without knowing his business thoroughly. Even the brightest Harvard MBA needs on-the-job training. Still, a corporation will do better if it confines itself and its acquisitions to a limited number of product lines. Most assuredly it should stay away from volatile, high technology. Even Xerox, with its great financial savvy and technological clout, failed with computers. It knew duplicating systems, not computers. It will be interesting, now, to see what IBM does with its copiers, but there's one important difference. IBM did not buy a copier company. Instead it developed a highly specialized line of products on its own.

But if you want to diversify, do it the way Beatrice Foods did it. Beginning as a dairy operation, Beatrice now includes furniture, graphics, chemicals, brushes, metal specialties, wearing apparel, sports goods, and luggage, plus an expanding line of foods. Two basic lessons can be learned from its success. First, buy only established, profitable companies and let them grow internally, without pouring in venture capital. Second, make sure that each acquisition has good entrepreneurial management, and let it operate the business as it did before the acquisition. The original management must have done something right. You bought its dream, didn't you?

Looking at the buyer's side more closely, we can list

factors that will help in following our two basic lessons.

1. *Financials.* Look beyond the cold, hard figures. Obviously, you and your people will review the seller's financials with an eagle eye. You may even try matching the company's five- or ten-year record against your own, or against your growth standards. But go further. Look at the seller's budgeting and accounting procedures, its standing with its bank, and certainly examine its management standards.

2. *The company structure.* Examine the seller's overall structure. Who set it up, how has it evolved over time? Don't be surprised to find no structure at all, but simply a hit-or-miss operation.

3. *Growth patterns.* Study growth programs and patterns. Have they been due to the industry's growth or to the seller's own aggressive savvy? How does its growth compare with other companies in its business? And did it follow through? Or has it grown through acquisition? If so, what kind of companies did it buy?

4. *Market position.* Nothing is more revealing about a company than its position in its marketplace. Is it the leader and if so, how did it get there? If not, where does it stand? Why did it fail to go further? Will your company help to move it upward?

5. *Standing with suppliers.* How does it relate to its basic suppliers and how do they feel about it? This tells a lot about a business, its management, and its standing in the business community. Some suppliers view a company as an easy touch; others will say it's a tough firm to deal with and respect it. A company that is strong with

its suppliers has a lot going for it and is always taken care of during shortages and price rises. Companies that aren't strong will be cut off first during shortages.

6. *Growth potential.* A company needs growth potential, not just a good record in the past. Careful, skillful study is needed here. Look at the company's creativity in product development.

7. *Reason for selling.* Again, why is the company for sale? Pinpoint the reasons and then dissect them from all angles. Will they affect you later—will they come back to haunt you?

8. *The seller's long-range objective.* The buyer wants to retain the seller's management if it can, but what are its management's own long-range goals? Do they match yours, or can they be made to match?

9. *The company's business philosophy.* Too few corporations look carefully enough at the seller's philosophy. Somehow, its acquisition team becomes too involved with financials, with contract details, with such things as executive remuneration, pension program changes, and so forth. Don't let it happen to you. As buyer, have a leisurely meeting with the seller's CEO and discuss his philosophy at length. Unless yours and his are compatible, the merger may well fail—unless it is understood from the beginning that you will put in your own management group.

10. *People evaluation.* Little is more significant than a company's management team. Evaluate fully your seller's team and carefully define the postmerger jobs of each member.

Chapter

6

Sexuality in a Merger

THERE REALLY IS sexuality in a merger—in a good merger or a bad one. In good ones there's the same excitement, the same anticipation of new but now mutual accomplishment, new growth, the same sense of well-being that comes from a good marriage. In a bad merger, as in a bad marriage, the result can be traumatic. Make no mistake: A merger is a marriage. You have to live with your new partner. If you can't you'll become so unhappy that some sort of separation, and probably a divorce, will take place, with all the frustration and guilt that goes with it.

It is vital, therefore, to select the proper partner *before* you get involved—before the courting, before the engagement, or even before you try a "meaningful relationship," corporate style. The wedding day is an anticlimax, compared with what went before. The settling down into day-to-day living, the conflicts and problems that begin

147

to show up—it happens in a merger. The once beautiful partner, with all those enticing curves, often turns out a shrew. The movie star groom becomes a pain in the neck. How do you know what you're getting? It is difficult and often impossible to know before signing on the dotted line, but you have to stop, look, and listen anyway. Let's look at a scenario and see what can happen. It begins this way.

The hard-working groom, serious and studious, has had his share of ups and downs, a few flings, a few encounters at singles' bars. Now he is ready for marriage, but not just any kind. Not out of infatuation, certainly not a marriage of convenience. What he has in mind is a beautiful, well-educated maiden, bright and lively, who can help build a happy, solid family. She will deal with all people in a tasteful, sophisticated way, as a hostess or guest, and will move comfortably among those of influence and affluence. She will be a good conversationalist. She will attract people with cultural as well as business bents. Women will like her for her friendliness, men not only for her beauty but for her maturity as a human being. Her background will have culture and wealth dating back several generations, yet her parents will appreciate the qualities that enabled a young man of lower station, but well educated and motivated, to succeed on his own, largely through discipline, hard work, and perseverance.

Where does one find such a bride, especially when the search has for so long been fruitless? Surely she exists. It is merely a matter of knowing where to look.

Talk it over with a good marriage broker, one who knows his way around and comes highly recommended.

After a careful survey of his own, the groom calls on Daniel Forthright Brightman. They meet for two hours and in the end the groom is confident that Dan is the man to help him. He has told him what he is looking for, and a lot about himself. Dan will now make a careful follow-up on several high-caliber candidates, each of whom meet the groom's criteria, and then report back with two specific recommendations. It should take about two weeks. The groom and Dan will discuss the potentialities of each and the groom will say which of the two Dan should approach first. Then marriage broker Dan will go to work, exploring the marriage potential with the bride's family first, and eventually with the bride herself. Dan and the groom settle on Dan's terms and conditions, whereupon Dan leaves with a promise to get going right away.

In ten days Dan telephones and with excitement says: "Have I got a bride for you!"

This does not sound quite like the serious, sincere Mr. Brightman the groom met, but after a few minutes he understands Dan's special enthusiasm, or he thinks he does.

"I have two delightful candidates for you but the one I am going to recommend is so beautiful and marvelous that I am positive you'll agree. In fact, because I'm so sure of it, and that my recommendation is so right for both of you, I felt I did not have to wait any longer. When shall we meet?" Next morning, they agreed.

That night, the groom hardly slept. All he could think of was his life ahead with a beautiful wife, new and exciting experiences, new people, new wealth, new appreciation of his special talents.

At eleven the next morning, friend Dan arrives quietly, identifying himself only as Mr. Brightman. The groom tells his secretary to hold all his calls—he wants no disturbance the next hour. Afterward they're going to lunch.

The meeting goes well. Friend Dan is cheerful and goes into greater detail on the bride, her background, her family. Liking what he hears, the groom asks Dan to arrange a meeting with the bride at an appropriate time and place.

"May I presume you have had some conversation with the bride or her parents?" the groom asks. "Yes and no," Dan replies. "I have talked with her parents but not with the bride herself. Her parents are very concerned about any marriage plans she might have, and particularly about the man she picks. This is a very delicate situation. I don't know what kind of person will actually fit the bill, but so far as I can tell you are the best candidate. I'll be talking to the bride's parents again and I'm sure everything will be arranged for an early, well-planned meeting. Leave it to me. I'll be in touch."

When the groom and bride finally meet, he is immediately captivated. She is beautiful, elegant, natural. They seem to have a great deal in common, and it is obvious to him that she likes him as much as he likes her. He asks for a second date and she accepts quickly.

A number of different endings could be written, now. At least one will be happy, another just so-so—a normal, routine marriage without much excitement, but still solid in a way. A third would be total disaster ending in divorce. Here's what happened.

The courtship went well and as the weeks passed the romance approached love. The bride liked the groom and showed it. The groom, in turn, was smitten with her beauty and charm. He also liked her parents, although without fully realizing it he was in awe of them, especially her father. Here was a man of real substance, he reasoned, who could help his career grow. Although the parents seemed to reciprocate his liking, they never really communicated with him. But for the groom it did not matter. His love for his darling was enough. It was almost a case of love at first sight.

So the marriage took place in the church of the bride's parents. Later there was a gala reception at their exclusive country club. It was all more than the groom and his own family had known, but it didn't really bother him. He gave it little thought. All he felt was admiration and love for his bride.

The honeymoon, a gift from the bride's parents, was perfect. Afterward, the happy couple moved into their new suburban home, spacious and fully furnished— another gift from the bride's affluent parents.

Then the fun started. It was not long before the bride's father, who said he saw potential for growth in the groom, began to direct his career openly. At first the groom thought of rebelling but after further thought (not very much) he acquiesced to the program the bride's strong, formal father laid out. Soon, however, he saw his mistake. By accepting his father-in-law's gifts, he also had to accept other things. It became clear he was no longer his own man and that his philosophy of life differed drastically from that of his in-laws—and even from his bride's. Funny, but as time went on she did not seem as beautiful, as romantic as she had.

No need to finish this scenario. The ending is self-evident, the point simple enough. Mergers, like marriages, can easily go on the rocks. Take my own case.

In March 1966 I met with a broker who had been after me for several years to sell our business. He had timed this meeting well. I had experienced several acquisition problems of my own and resolved them. Now as president and chief executive of the company I founded in 1944, I was publishing eight fairly small business magazines and several other periodicals, directories, and newsletters. Our annual sales amounted to $2.5 million. We were profitable but not greatly so, mainly because we were continually launching a new magazine or repairing a run-down one we had acquired, which may have helped our growth but not our earnings.

Then 58 years old, I owned 80 percent of our business but had begun to ask myself where I was going. What business, career plans should I have for the years ahead? If I joined up with a large public company with a mandatory retirement program, I would have only about eight productive years more, even though I was in good health and, more importantly, enjoyed what I was doing.

Nevertheless, I had to conclude that what I most wanted was to accelerate our growth. The best way to do it was to merge with a prestigious, well-financed, charismatic public communications corporation, one with no business magazine operation but wanting to acquire one.

The broker and I met at lunch and, continuing in my office, we reviewed a list of potential marriage partners. We both decided that Cowles Communications, Inc. would be ideal for us—and we for Cowles. Its latest annual report revealed an enviable ten-year record. Sales and profits were increasing yearly, and annual volume at that time was close to $200 million, net earnings close to $10 million. It was involved in almost every area of communications from electronic media to newspapers and periodicals—everything except business and professional magazines. From his exploratory talks with Cowles's president, my broker believed they did want to enter the business and professional magazine area, and by acquisition. He had also explained that our company would be the ideal way to do it, plus a great opportunity for me and my young, able, motivated team of managers to increase our own growth. And of course it would provide me with a significant capital gains opportunity in Cowles stock, cash, or both. I agreed we should pursue it.

After settling on terms and the basic price we would ask, I authorized him to meet again with Marvin Whatmore, Cowles's president, to discuss the marriage seriously. Having known my broker, a specialist in communications mergers, for some time, I felt he knew what I was after as well as I did: A chance to build a large, profitable publishing operation, with a goal of $50 million in revenue and at least $5 to $8 million in net profit.

In a few hours my broker called me back. He was seeing Mr. Whatmore the next morning. Shortly before lunch the next day he telephoned again, this time excitedly. "Don, I think we will have a deal. Mr. Whatmore is very enthusiastic about the prospects for a merger with your company and you. Cowles had been thinking of getting into the business magazine field for some time and about six months ago they came close to buying one of the larger companies in this area. Now it appears they prefer a smaller firm, with good management that would include a highly motivated chief executive who could build a substantial business magazine division. You fit the bill just perfectly."

I met Marvin Whatmore for lunch several days later, when he was my guest in my club. The chemistry seemed right. He asked for our financials and within a week negotiations began in earnest. With his executive associates, Mr. Whatmore, charismatic and friendly, started romancing me. He invited my wife and me to Sunday brunch at his beautiful Westchester County estate. I knew it was to give some of the more important Cowles officers and key executives a chance to look me over, and although I felt slightly ill at ease, I enjoyed being romanced. Several of the Cowles people impressed me, one or two I did not particularly care for, but overall they seemed a good and friendly group. Although Chairman Gardner Cowles and Mrs. Cowles were not there, I met them later, first at a gala opening at the Museum of Modern Art and again at an informal-formal luncheon in the Cowles Executive Dining Room. He awed me, I admit. He was a legend in magazine and newspaper editing and publishing. I felt young, the product of a respectable but not really good family, about to marry the beautiful daughter of rich, socially important parents. I was walking on air.

We started to draw up contracts toward the end of June. Discussions continued and so did the romancing. The wedding day was not scheduled until late November, but so sure and enthusiastic about the marriage did everyone feel that I was elected to the board of directors of Cowles Communications, Inc. several weeks before it. There were more lunches, more people to meet—people who would be my new family. Nice people, those, I thought, and I became friends with several.

Yes, I did fairly well in developing my contract, but I also made several mistakes along the way. I wasn't self-confident enough. To a certain extent I depended a little too much on the advice of the special attorney I selected to help our own corporate lawyer, who seemed more in awe of the Cowles people than even I. I settled for less than I should have insisted on, especially in the matter of my salary and other remuneration. I was just a little afraid that if I pushed too hard I might blow the entire deal. But it was a satisfactory deal, basically, in the price I got and the position I would have in the Cowles hierarchy. I was to be president of the newly formed Cowles

Business and Professional Magazine Division, with a seat on the board and a number of other valuable perks. So I signed on the dotted line.

The honeymoon lasted the better part of two years—long in a corporate marriage—largely because I was busy buying companies and magazines. Within two years, I built my division's volume to $12.5 million with pretax profits of $2.5 million. It seemed I was on the way to my goal of $50 million in sales and $5 to $8 million in profits.

However, as I was doing my thing and doing it well, a series of unhappy developments occurred in other divisions of the corporation. Some started losing money. As a member of the board of directors, I knew what was happening to the company I had married—all for stock, which was declining. I saw a good marriage turning sour and there was little I could do to sweeten it. I made sounds at board meetings but the boss wouldn't listen. He was annoyed with my remarks and proposals, actually, so I did the only thing that seemed logical. I moved to extricate myself from the upcoming corporate disaster by offering to buy my company back. After a year I succeeded, but that's another story. (I tell it in *Divorce Corporate Style*.)

The thing to remember is that if mergers are marriages, look carefully before courting. Look coldly, objectively, and don't sign until you're sure you've seen everything. Even so, there's a chance you'll be disappointed. But just as there are happy marriages, successful mergers do exist. The game *can* have a happy ending.

Chapter

7

Do You Really Want to Sell Your Business?

SUPPOSE YOU HAVE SPENT weeks, months, maybe a year, discussing or negotiating the sale of your company. A lot of it has been stimulating. You have a good gut feeling about your prospective buyer and its key executives, but you also have some doubts. They keep creeping into your mind during odd moments, or when you wake up at four in the morning thinking about the merger. You have spent a good part of your life building the company, and it is successful at last. Year after year it has made money. You feel fulfilled. Best of all, you like what you are doing. You are your own man and you enjoy the freedom.

Why, then, do you want to sell your company? For

one thing, your attorney and your accountant keep repeating that if anything should happen to you (why don't they just say: If you die? *When* you die?) your family would have difficulty selling it. Merely to meet the tax burden they might even have to sell at a sacrifice price. It may not be a one-man operation, but your company is still worth more during your life than after.

You buy all of this, sure, but you also think: I did not start my business to make a fortune for my family. My wife will be taken care of financially no matter what happens; insurance and my other investments will be more than adequate. My children? They are doing well enough on their own. My son, the doctor, has no money problems now and will do even better later. My son, the professor, earns a nice living and enjoys college life in California. My daughter is married to a corporate executive. He is moving up, so who knows? He might take the business over (but he has made plain that he has his own ideas on his future). At any rate, no financial problems there, either.

Well, why *do* you want to sell?

The answer is, you don't want to SELL it. You really want to MERGE with a prestigious, long-established, well-financed public company to accelerate your own growth. Until now you have grown internally, but to really expand will take capital, many times more than you have or can borrow. With the stock of a listed public company and its financial clout, prospects could be limitless.

Still those doubts—even in your dreams. You feel

ambivalent. Maybe you should break off altogether? But again, they are good people and you may miss a great opportunity.

So what do you do?

Arrange a meeting with the principals you like and have talked with. Explain in advance that you have a new plan to put before them; then prepare yourself fully with all of the information you'll need on it. The plan is called Meaningful Relationship Corporate Style.

It would be a good idea to meet at your own luncheon club or at your own favorite restaurant, but don't talk about your plan until after lunch. Say that you like the company and the people, especially those with whom you have been negotiating. Also that you like the merger concept. Still, you're not sure you want to give up control of your company *at this time*. Why not an interlocking arrangement—an engagement—which eventually would lead to marriage? It's a meaningful relationship and could look like this:

You sell them a minority interest in your business—no more than 25 percent, or whatever will keep you with full control. One or more of their executives will be elected to your board of directors, but the majority will still be your own nominees, of course. A five-year working agreement will be formulated by which you give the corporation "first refusal" on your company under predetermined conditions and pricing formula.

The agreement signed, you will move to buy other companies yourself, the ones you have had your own eye on for some time. They will be bought with the corporation's stock, cash, or both, and of course the corporation will own them. The corporation will form a new subsidiary to encompass them but you and your associates will manage their affairs, with you as president or general manager. Naturally, the companies you buy will be congeneric with your own business but will represent a new line or area of interest, the way your business is new to the corporation.

You, your associates, or your company will receive a management fee for operating the new subsidiary under a five-year management contract. You will also get a percentage (say 10 to 20) of the subsidiary's improved net earnings, cumulative over the contract's life. At the end of that period or before, as agreed upon by both parties, you may decide to sell your company (or what you own of it) to the corporation under a "first refusal" provision. Your company will then merge with the company or companies you acquired for the subsidiary and which you managed successfully. You, of course, will continue as chief executive or general manager of the combined operation by a contract satisfactory to both parties in salary, incentives, time, and other conditions.

Or, if you decide not to sell control of your company your meaningful relationship will end. You buy back the minority interest, which you had sold, and everything terminates amicably.

The advantages in all this should be obvious to both parties. No one has much to lose but a lot to gain. You, however, can learn through experience whether it's really for you, whether the sale of your business is really what you want, and whether you'll be able to adjust to it later if you do sell. Likewise the buyers. They'll learn whether you and your associates can really make a significant contribution to the growth of the corporation—especially by buying new businesses successfully and managing them well.

Naturally, the corporation can approve or reject any acquisition you may want or initiate. Here the real test of compatibility will come, and early in the relationship. The executive team will get a fairly clear idea whether the companies you want are the kind that make sense in the long run for the corporation. You in turn will learn just as quickly whether you will get the cooperation from them that you expect and need, and whether your acquisition philosophy really matches theirs. It could either be one beautiful satisfaction or a pile of frustrations.

On the surface, this plan may appear farfetched. It is certainly unusual and to my knowledge it has never been tried, but for some sellers and buyers it is worth thinking about seriously. With some modifications for special needs in particular situations, the meaningful relationship—or trial marriage—could work.

Of course there are other ways besides merging to secure capital gains for yourself and to protect your estate. One of the most obvious is to go public, but this too is fraught with dangers and can be costly. All types of businesses—start ups, highly speculative outfits, companies with losses instead of profits—could and did do this in the sizzling sixties. Some of the lesser ones did it on the "best effort" basis of minor underwriters, many of whom have since gone bankrupt (a few others were convicted of fraud). But all this has changed. Since 1970, the public market for small, speculative, unprofitable companies has dried up. With some of the highly rated, better known, successful shares selling at five to ten times earnings, who needs to buy a risky new public issue?

Nevertheless, one thing about going public, especially for a profitable growth company, is that it gives you your cake while you're eating it. You can sell only a minority portion of your shares to the public—say, from 10 to 40 percent—and keep the rest. Use some of the proceeds for the business and keep the rest in hard cash for yourself and your associates. The stock you retain will now have a public market, and in time could be traded on the big board.

Let's look at it step by step. The first step is planning. Put your house in order. Structure your company to maximize its profits and in doing so make sure you keep working control. Meet with your attorney and accountant and tell them your plans. If they lack experience in taking clients public, suggest they retain another firm that has it. They may do it voluntarily, but if not raise the matter yourself. Your attorney and accountant will meet to coordinate the legal and accounting matters among themselves, then with you. Now, with their help and your commercial bank's, structure or restructure your setup to position it best for a public issue. If necessary combine your corporations into one. Next, have a preliminary discussion with an underwriter, but make sure you have good numbers to show him—a record of earnings growth going back at least five years, with equally good projections for the next five.

It is important, here, to note that the quality and standing of the underwriter is vital to your success, but the best, well-capitalized ones, with the best connections, can afford to be very selective. If your annual sales are around $50 million and net earnings in the millions, almost any of these will take you on, and you may even have your pick. If your sales are between $10 and $20 million and profits are less than a million, however, your chances are minimal. Still, there are good and successful second- or third-line underwriters to call on. (If your sales are less than $10 million and profits marginal, forget about going public altogether, unless you have an unusual product—one with an explosive profit potential, given the right development, plant, and capital.)

But whatever you do, don't shop around and don't accept an underwriter that's clearly fourth-rate. Your commercial bank, your accountant, and your attorney can help. Your own brokerage firm, if it handles your corporate or personal investments, may also be underwriting new issues, or could recommend one that is. The point is, once word gets around Wall Street that you are shopping, your chance of finding the prestigious firm you want will be lessened. It is, as we said, a club, and you'll have to play by its rules. If the underwriter you are talking with decides that your company is not big enough for its operation, it may recommend or put you in touch with a smaller, equally capable one. When a first-line underwriter recommends or actually helps you select a

THE NEW MERGER GAME

smaller house, you can be reasonably certain you have a winner.

Once you have your underwriter the work really begins. You talk, consult, discuss with your attorneys and accountants—and talk, consult, discuss some more. There seems to be no other way. Sure, you can leave everything to your professionals, but my advice is to stay on top of it yourself. Know what is happening, how, and why. Most important, know what it will really mean for you and your business.

The next step is preparing the prospectus—the "red herring." If your corporation cannot stand full public disclosure, or if you can't meet requirements set by the SEC, you might as well stop right here. The expenses of drawing up, printing, and submitting your prospectus to the SEC can be very high—and you will be paying the bills. They can run $50,000 or more, and if an underwriting does not take place you and your business will lose it.

Another thing. In setting up an underwriting situation make sure it is not a "best effort" deal. "Best effort" commits the underwriters to sell only a part, sometimes a very small part, of the total offering. Instead, make sure that your underwriting is guaranteed all or none. The managing underwriter, or group, acquires a control of the total offering, allotting the balance of shares for sale by other underwriters or brokers. If any are unsold in the initial offering, they are bought by your underwriters themselves, but you are paid for the entire issue at the agreed price per share, less underwriters' commission.

This can take a year or longer. Even under the best

circumstances, an underwriting usually cannot be completed in less than six months. The SEC alone can take two to six months to clear your prospectus. And all the while you have a business to run—which is not easy. Your mind is being diverted, constantly, to the underwriting, and all the other details and problems. Taking a company public is only for the strong-hearted, for those with guts.

But there's another alternative to a merger or sale. This is a joint venture, or an arrangement generally referred to as a "cooperation agreement," both of which flourished during the past few years. Basically, two companies agree to form a jointly owned operation intended to finance, produce, market, and promote a new product or product line, to explore new product ideas.

Let's say you own and operate a small or medium-size company. You have had a little growth and you are profitable when an idea with vast potential occurs to you, or you develop a product line that could expand your business significantly. There is just one problem. Your new idea, your new product line is so ambitious that to attempt to put it across yourself or with a commercial bank loan could jeopardize the capital structure of your entire business, if not bankrupt it altogether. You need capital and talent and you don't have them. You know this for certain but you also know that to put the idea or the product aside would be a total waste. You would be losing an opportunity that might not come again.

Here is where a joint venture makes sense. You offer to share this new creation with another corporation, usually one that is well financed and much larger than yours. The extent of the sharing will depend on capital requirements, the facilities needed, and the time required to bring the idea and product to fruition and profitability. Ideally you want control of the joint venture company yourself, but this is not likely. You'd settle for a fifty-fifty arrangement, but unless you can offer your own capital and talent, even this is unlikely. Still, if you only get a 40, 25, or merely 10 percent ownership it may be worthwhile. A 10 percent share in a venture with a large, well-capitalized public company whose management will back it to the hilt can sometimes turn out to be more than your total original business.

For example, in 1975 the Rouse Co., of Columbia, Maryland, with several million in sales and net earnings of about $200,000, initiated a joint venture with Federated Stores Realty, Inc., a subsidiary of the multibillion dollar Federated Department Stores, Inc., to develop a retail center in Fort Worth, Texas. The idea and approach came from Rouse, but obviously the financing came from Federated, which also set the stores up and managed them.

To me, this is a more practical way for small or medium-size companies to go about it, better than the venture capital route. Venture capitalists, with few exceptions, lack operating talent and experience. Rather, they are financial people looking for a killing. They demand a huge portion—often control—of a business in return for their capital, and very often they'll ruin it.

A cooperation arrangement, different from a joint

venture, involves a licensing agreement to produce and sell a product or line. These have become popular for American corporations doing business internationally, particularly in oil producing countries, but they also work well with large and small operations domestically.

Take the agreement concluded in 1974 between the then $2 billion General Dynamics Corp. and the small Penril Corp. of Rockville, Maryland, whose sales were slightly over $4 million with net profits of about $600,000. Penril worked out a three-year cooperation agreement whereby its Data Communications Division received "authorization" to lease data products to General Dynamics's facilities in North America. This proved to be a good deal for Penril as well as General Dynamics. Penril's Data Communications Division has been successful in doing considerable leasing of its data products to General Dynamics, and the three-year contract is being renewed. Sales of Penril have increased to $10 million, largely as a result of its cooperation arrangement with General Dynamics and similar agreements with a number of other companies.

Or take a different type of agreement signed in 1975 by Fingerhut Corporation and Daystro-Scientific. Fingerhut, a direct mail merchandiser with sales of $300 million but whose profits of about a million dollars were marginal, agreed to market jointly a Daystro medical injection device.

One of the newer methods corporations use to provide capital gains for their principal stockholders is the employee stock ownership plan, ESOP. The founder and pioneer of ESOP is Louis Kelso. He has been trying to sell the idea, especially to private, closely held corporations, for some time but not until several years ago did he begin making progress. Among his more active supporters now is Senator Russell Long of Louisiana.

What is an ESOP? Based on a legalistic explanation in the November 1975 *American Bar Association Journal*, it is a trust established to hold stock for employees. In some ways it resembles the familiar profit-sharing plan, in that the stock is normally distributed to each employee in the plan on his or her retirement or termination—in effect as deferred compensation. Because the trust invests only in stock of the employees' own company, through non-recourse borrowing guaranteed by the company, it gives employees a piece of their own action. The trust at a later period repays the debt, usually to a commercial bank, with company contributions to the trust deductible.

Currently, ESOPs are being used by principals of a private company who liquidate their positions in it for cash, using before-tax dollars instead of after-tax dollars of the company. Owners of privately owned corporations thus obtain capital gains through the sale of their stock to the ESOP, while employees in effect buy it, giving them now a personal interest in their outfit and special incentive to help it succeed. The basic difference between an ESOP and a profit-sharing trust is that an ESOP invests solely in its own company's stock, while profit-sharing trusts normally invest in other companies. Also, an ESOP's distributions to employees are in stock, not cash, and the company's contributions to its ESOP need not come solely from its profits. Finally, the ESOP may also be used as a financing vehicle, receiving bank loans guaranteed by the company or its shareholder employees. For owners or principals in closely held corporations, there are other benefits to ESOPs. They can be used to establish for estate taxes the value of their stock. ESOPs may also be used to fund buy-and-sell agreements, including agreements effective at demise and possibly those funded by deductible, key-man insurance premiums.

The number of other opportunities for capital gains in the closely held corporation is practically limitless, and the owner who is doubtful about merging should know them. He could sell his real estate or other holdings to his corporation. There are also various kinds of trusts and foundations. Just be certain you understand and can live with them later, and that they meet IRS and other legal requirements. You must not only study your estate planning options carefully, but you need an experienced estate attorney and tax person. If you wish, work with the trust department of your bank, but work with your lawyer and accountant too. Depending on a bank's trust department alone is dangerous. Too, make sure your pension program has been properly adjusted, or rewritten, to conform to the new ERISA (Employee Retirement Income Security Act), that you understand the implications, costs, and benefits, and how it fits into your own estate program. The new breed of pension planning consultants can be valuable. Company-paid insurance also fits here. The owner can be a wife, child, or grandchild, or other family members, or it can be your corporation. In that case you can develop a program, outside of ESOP, whereby your surviving key executives would have funds to buy your stock. Or, consider a stock-voting trust to remove the stock of your closely held business from your estate, while you retain control over the corporation.

The purpose of these comments is not to offer legal, accounting, or tax advice—your own professionals are to be consulted for such needs—but to suggest a practical, down to earth guide, a good part of which is based on experience and the rest on research. The one element to guard against is losing control of your business while you are setting up estate programs, developing a plan to dispose of your business if and when you decide on retirement or semiretirement, or establishing a program whereby the business will be sold to a group of your able and trusted employees after your demise. I repeat, in any such programs, make certain that you continue to control your business as long as you want to. Another thing to remember: In programs involving estate planning but especially when the situation calls for the sale of your business to able, deserving employees on your retirement or death, liquidity is paramount. Make sure there will be enough cash in your treasury to help your selected employees buy control of your business, so that your wife and other heirs will receive what you consider its true value in the form of cash or securities. A good, solid balance sheet can be of tremendous help, not only in the form of cash and marketable securities but in needed bank credit for your business survivors.

Finally, remember that no matter what professional talent you consult to aid you in setting up the program of your desire, you owe it to yourself to understand every possible element of that program. Not only is this good business, but you will feel better for it.

Chapter

8

Rules of the Merger Game

HERE ARE SOME concerns that will help everyone avoid problems before the merger—and worse problems later.

1. Have you defined your postmerger role? Without a clear understanding of what it will be, your management team could be devastated. In some extreme circumstances, it could also kill you and everything you worked to build.

Develop an agreement—usually an employment contract—that specifies your title, your function, your responsibility, your authority, your management limitations, your salary and incentives, your place in the chain of command. It will include the term of your employment and usually your options for renewal. It will also define the terms of dismissal and resignation, and what you may or may not do then. You must decide for yourself what you want and it is then up to your attorney, after everyone agrees, to put it into concise legal language.

2. Should you go onto the board of directors of the corporation with which you are merging your company? Assuming you are invited, or you ask and they consent, what does it mean?

From the psychological and public relations point of view, it means a lot. You feel important and look important to your friends, your industry, the financial community, and your bank. But what does it mean from a pragmatic, constructive viewpoint? Not very much. You're a minority, just one of ten, fifteen, or more. Even if you own a big chunk of stock, your power will be limited. The chief executive normally controls the board. Each member is elected yearly, at the company's annual meeting, which means you are all there at the CEO's pleasure. Sure, you can voice your opinions at board meetings, but chances are that if they are contrary to those of the chief executive and his executive committee, they will not be worth much. Persist, and you will be considered a crank. Ideas of a constructive nature can be presented more effectively to your CEO person to person, whether you are a member of the board or not. At any rate, when it comes to voting on resolutions, it will be aye for you, not nay, and for other board members too, or you will all be off the board at the next annual meeting. The chairman has the votes, so the best you can do is sit silently. If he didn't, neither he nor the board could function.

But there are some harsher negatives to board membership. You and the others are liable for all the board's actions—that is, for all major corporate decisions. The corporation insures you against law suits, but there are other, equally serious liabilities. If you are a substantial stockholder you are considered an "insider." This means you are subject to the SEC's Rule 144. Within any six-month period you may not sell more than one percent of the shares outstanding, or more than the average weekly volume of shares traded during the four weeks preceding your sell order, whichever is less. A restriction like this can place you in a serious bind if the price of your stock begins to fall sharply. You may not be able to sell more than a tiny portion.

3. Do you know what will happen to your pension program? Your own company probably has a pension plan, good for you and your employees. The corporation you're joining may have one too, but is it as good? If you are going to exchange your plan for your parent's be sure it's as generous, or more generous, than yours, or insist on staying with what you've got. Consider your employees as well, and of course the effect of ERISA.

4. What about profit sharing? The corporation into which you are merging has a profit-sharing program and you are invited to join. Great. Just don't exchange your superior pension program for their profit sharing. Try to get both, but if for legal or policy reasons you must choose one or the other, keep your own program. If profits decline or if there aren't any for several years, you could lose plenty.

5. Have the expansion plans for your company as a

subsidiary or division of the larger outfit been defined? Get your new partner's intentions on the table at the outset, or expect to be stymied and frustrated later.

6. What will happen to your present executives and employees? This is vital. Most of your people are good and you want them to remain. It is up to you to establish their new roles. Of course, you will also identify your own backup, and you will eliminate some of the duds you've been carrying for mostly humane reasons. This is a good chance to do it as painlessly as possible.

7. Where will your office and plant be? Unless you have good reasons not to, better stay where you are, at least for the foreseeable future. You'll need time to digest your new corporate food and it may give you heartburn.

8. What about the duration of your new employment contract? Only you can answer that but it is extremely important. Some sellers want no employment contract at all. They plan to continue as operating heads of their subsidiaries or divisions, but they also want to be free to quit if things are not to their liking. My advice: Negotiate a workable agreement intended to last three to five years, but with renewal options and sensible provisions for "outs" by both sides.

9. What do you want from your new corporate headquarters? Your new parent has facilities for marketing and product research. They can be yours for constructive use. There's also executive talent. Discuss these, and how and at what price you will be able to utilize them.

On the other hand, while you expect constructive

supervision, you should not have to endure downright interference from your parent. Specify what you want and don't want from headquarters. You may not get it all, but airing your needs and expectations before the merger can help avoid misunderstandings later.

For example, what will happen to your accounting department? Plenty. It will be merged or coordinated with its headquarters counterpart and many technicalities, such as the effect of pooling interest, will be considered. Expect adjustments. Your present chief accounting officer, if he is exceptional and adaptable, may keep his job, but report to someone higher—or he may be replaced. At any rate, you will no longer be boss of accounting, which will now be just a link in a longer chain. To avoid misunderstandings, again clear the air beforehand. Remember too that the auditing firm you have used you will use no longer. A completely new team, probably one of the Big Eight, will take over.

10. What if the merger does not work? Despite good intentions and big plans for the future, it may not. Let's say the corporation decides it no longer wants to be in your division's business. What happens to you then? You have a contract, of course, and the corporation will probably honor it, or may try to buy it out. This may be satisfactory to you, but what are your other options? The corporation may sell your division to another company, with you and your contract. Or it may spin you off. Your division would then be a public company with you as president.

What if your division is sold and you don't like the

deal? Why not buy back your division and again operate independently? If that's your wish, start negotiating quickly, before word gets around that your division is being peddled, and you may well make a good deal. You will need financing, of course, in which case your pre-merger commercial or investment banker could help, or you might sell some of your stock in the parent corporation. You may even invite your key or up-and-coming people to join in the buyback, making your reacquired company wholly employee-owned, with you in control. Try it on a payout basis, or have the buyback financed by your commercial bank, at least in part; but however you do it, try to keep a small nest egg in stock or cash outside the business. The security will be important. In the end, the decision and the methods will be up to you and only you.

11. Put a bottom price on your stock. This may be last on our list but it is first in importance. You decide to take common stock for your company in a tax-free exchange merger. Your buyer is successful and prestigious. It has an excellent, even spectacular, ten-year growth record with sales and profits increasing handsomely year after year. The stock has been split at least once, perhaps twice, during the past decade, and seems fairly priced now at 18 times earnings. What have you got to worry about? Plenty.

Anything can happen to this marvelous growth company, and to the price of its stock, because anything can happen to the market. Comes a recession or for no reason at all, really, your shares in your parent drop to six times earnings. The $3 million you received for your business is now worth $1 million. We've seen some of the best companies, such as Polaroid Corp., go from $135 a share to $12. Look what happened to Avon, Disneyland, IBM, Xerox, General Motors, Chrysler, Litton, and others, not to mention the stock of lesser corporations. Thus, one way to protect yourself is to insist on a floor for the price of the stock you are getting. If the buyer wants your company badly enough, you will get it. You can agree that if the price of the stock drops sharply, you will be issued additional shares in compensation. How many is up for negotiation and agreement by your parent. It's not an unreasonable request, but neither is it a routine one. Check your lawyers and accountants. SEC rules and other regulations change with time, and you may have to make different arrangements.

More advice. No matter how good your advisers are, read the contract carefully before you sign it. Make sure that everything you agreed upon is there in the final draft. Ask about anything you do not understand or are unsure of, but don't be a nitpicker. It will waste time and probably irritate everybody. What you care about are the basics.

Now for the signing, probably in your new parent's board room. Don't expect cheers or champagne. It's merely a formality, after so many months of negotiations, and it will seem anticlimactic. You leave the room and as you start back to your office, you have a strange feeling of ambivalence. You feel great, sure. You are rich, the owner of several million dollars in marketable securities, and head of a valuable division of a respected public company. But you also feel a pang. Your baby, the child you have loved, trained, and nurtured through illness and trouble to adulthood, is no longer yours alone. Worse, although you tried not to think about it, you awake fully to the fact you are now an employee. Important though you are, you still work for someone else. The feeling may fade but it never disappears. It will return again, often in those hours before dawn.

Now you dig into the things you deferred during the long negotiations. In a few days the publicity is written (by your new PR man, with your approval of course) and published. Your ebullience and doubts have given way to lassitude, maybe sheer exhaustion. Still you begin to return to normal, slowly. You begin to adjust. But now, as president or general manager or whatever, how should you behave?

If you defined your new role successfully before the merger, you should know your functions and responsibilities. Go back to work. Decide on the personnel changes you want to make and after advising the executive you report to, make them. You're still running your division and the responsibilities are yours. Advise and inform headquarters but don't ask approval. Headquarters wants you to run your own operation, essentially. It bought a successful company, managed by an able chief executive who knows its policies. The less you run to headquarters the better. All that is expected is that your sales and especially your profits continue upward. The bottom line counts most.

But if headquarters wants something from you, you will hear about it. When your boss requests a visit, ask the purpose and then set a date as convenient for you as for him. Just make sure that when you get there you are prepared. If unexpected questions arise and you can't answer them precisely, admit it without hesitation. Say you will develop the answers in reasonable time, but promise nothing you cannot deliver. It will earn you the respect you deserve. There is absolutely no reason to be nervous. Remember, no one at headquarters knows as much about your business as you do.

On matters of capital expenditure or investment, especially if the amounts are substantial, do not make decisions unilaterally. Present your major capital needs to headquarters for approval. Answer critical questions fully and have all background ready. Most public corporations involved in mergers and acquisitions have set policies with regard to such things, but subsidiary managers do not need an okay for the routine purchases, such as for replacement and normal inventory, although there may be budgeted ceilings. If need for big expenditures arises, be prepared to develop a full factual case. Approval will probably be forthcoming but it may take longer than you think it should. Have patience. This is the way in the big corporate structure. If speed is crucial, however, and you make it known, authorization will come quicker. But whatever you do, do it courteously yet firmly.

So your merger is off to a good start and the road ahead looks clear. What assurance do you have it will continue? None. No one ever does completely. Still, there are a number of things you can do on your own to help it along.

Let's say that life, the way things are done, in your new corporation, or in the divisions you're familiar with, appears lavish, richer, more expensive. Your associates and other employees notice it too. Something strange begins happening. Until the merger you ran a tight ship (one reason you were successful), but without your realizing it things now loosen up. You are so busy with meetings at headquarters that you no longer watch your division's costs as closely. Excesses and errors appear in purchasing, and more clerks than are necessary. Attendance rules are not observed carefully. Your management is traveling first class and entertaining sumptuously. The worst thing is, you are not aware that so much waste has occurred until you hear about it, not from one of your own executives, but from someone at headquarters who got word from accounting there. Do not let this happen to you. Set your division's operating policy yourself at the start and make it clear right down to middle management. Now more than ever you have to watch costs. You are expected to improve the bottom line, not worsen it, and you can't do this without an operation that is as tight after the merger as it was before.

Your next big project is to begin negotiating for the company you had your eye on long before your own merger. It is a bigger operation, but you know you are now in an excellent position to bring it in, enabling you to leapfrog to new heights. What is your approach?

Discuss it with the people at headquarters with whom you have developed a close working relationship. It will take several meetings before you receive the go-ahead, but with that and all the research backup headquarters can give you, make the initial move. You have gone through it yourself, but there are at least two essentials to consider and observe to the letter.

The first is to offer a fair, reasonable price but no more than you would have offered when you were independent. You are now headquarters and headquarters is your company. Also, you will deal with the sellers in the courteous but businesslike manner you expected that headquarters would use in dealing with you. Sounds like elementary stuff, but it is not.

The second essential has special sophistication. You are buying a larger operation, perhaps four or five times larger, and maybe it's older and more prestigious. Don't let this floor you, but do make it clear from the beginning, to everyone including headquarters, that you will be in charge. This bigger company will be merged into yours and together, but under your management, you will both grow. This is important. Otherwise, its owners—headquarters—could labor under the misapprehension that your operation will merge into theirs and that their management will prevail. You cannot let this happen. You have sought the firm, perceived the opportunities, set the price. Now you establish the policy and the tone. No matter that your unit is smaller. You merged your company with headquarters, and you must make clear that you intend to stay Number One in the combined operation.

This is not an easy task. It requires judicious handling and a sound knowledge of psychology. It also requires careful timing. You have to know the marketplace and whether the merger movement generally is on the upswing. Does the company have special growth potential? Is the CEO or founder aging, or does he have estate problems? Does he need special financing? And what about the overall economy? All of these are matters of timing. Effective timing will help the buyer avoid duds, companies on the decline and beyond revival. It will keep him from entering an industry at the top of its growth cycle, with no place to go but down, or entering one long before its breakout. The same holds true for the seller. Timing is crucial.

Sure, in your first acquisition use everything headquarters has to offer, but do it under your own direction and with full knowledge. Don't lose control. Buying the company is your responsibility—but it is also a terrific opportunity to demonstrate what you can do in a situation of this kind. It could be a valuable first step in your growth with headquarters.

Chapter

9

You Can Make It Big with Headquarters

YOU'VE COMPLETED your first big acquisition and dovetailed it successfully with your organization. It is entirely possible that headquarters will ask you to help with other mergers and acquisitions. For you this is an important step, a sign you have been recognized as potentially top executive material. If you are young enough and sufficiently adaptable to new and untried situations, you'll probably want this. Although the head of an independent, merged company doesn't often move up in the headquarters hierarchy, in some rare instances he'll go right to the top.

Corporate politics aside, the need for managerial talent is considerable and sought avidly by the large, listed public corporation. A few interesting examples show that executives of acquired companies can make it with their new headquarters, and also show some of the whys and hows of their success.

Take Dick Gelb. In 1958 Richard L. Gelb was 35 and president of the family-owned Clairol Co. Founded by his father, Lawrence, almost by accident, Clairol was an up-and-coming, smartly promoted cosmetic operation when it merged into Bristol-Myers Co., the expansion-minded pharmaceutical company. Though public and listed, Bristol-Myers was still under control by the Bristol family. Annual sales were only slightly more than $100 million, but its management, then headed by able CEO Gavin MacBain, had big plans for the future. These, he knew, depended on new product lines and exceptional executive talent. Acquiring Clairol and the talents of several of the Gelbs seemed an excellent way to go about it, despite the fact that with annual sales of $18 million Clairol was not very large either. What attracted Bristol-Myers was its potential in product, marketing, and management. Strangely, neither Dick nor his younger brother, Bruce, wanted any part of a sale—to Bristol-Myers or any other company—but despite their strong opposition, father Lawrence overruled them and went ahead. He sold Clairol to Bristol-Myers for cash— $22.5 million of it. Once the "merger" was completed, however, they went along and assumed managerial roles in what was now the Clairol Division. Credit for this must be given to Gavin MacBain, who engineered the deal. Not only did Gavin see vast potential in Clairol, he also saw it in the Gelbs, particularly Dick.

Gavin's judgment proved correct. It turned out to be a perfect, delightful marriage. Dick continued as division president and moved quickly into the headquarters hierarchy, first as corporate vice-president and in a few years as president. Gavin MacBain became chairman and remained chief executive officer until 1972, when Dick Gelb took over. Gavin MacBain continued as chairman while Dick's younger brother, Bruce, moved up into Clairol's presidency. Through Dick's efforts Bristol-Myers has become a $2 billion business, with Clairol alone accounting for $500 million in annual volume.

How did Dick Gelb do it? Not by pushing his weight around. (The Gelb family eventually became substantial B-M stockholders by buying on the open market, and today Dick is among B-M's biggest.) He merely ran Clairol intelligently, advertising and marketing its products creatively. Profits grew as product mix expanded and marketing effort was enlarged. At the same time he accepted new challenges and opportunities from headquarters. Tall, handsome, well tailored and groomed (he prefers to let his hair become gray instead of darkening it with a Clairol product), Dick is essentially a quiet, reserved, private, and basically shy person. He does not seek publicity and in fact tries to avoid it, except where the company's image might benefit. He is, however, a strong, tough, highly competitive manager.

Interestingly, instead of directing Bristol-Myers toward greater emphasis on cosmetics, he moved into pharmaceuticals. He realized from the beginning of the merger that here was a field with much bigger opportu-

he company merged into the corporation and he should try to be flexible enough to be able to adjust to the needs of his new environment."

I then commented: "About 30 years ago Bud Schulberg wrote a novel called *What Makes Sammy Run?* Sammy, the character, personified the upcoming, pushy, 'let-no-one-stand-in-my-way' business executive of that time. How would you describe today's upcoming professional business executive?" His answer: "He is the very opposite, 180 degrees removed, from the type of a manager described in *What Makes Sammy Run?*"

"Why do most executives of private companies in a merger situation fail?"

"They are more concerned with themselves than the needs of the corporation. And they do not learn quickly enough. They do not do their homework well," he replied.

I changed the subject. "Charlie Revson hired so many able executives and then fired them. The Revlon executive suite, expensively but attractively carpeted and furnished and surrounded by beautiful and elegant secretaries, turned out to be the proverbial revolving door. Thus, he never really selected a successor to himself until your appointment. Why did he pick you?"

He smiled. "As a matter of fact, I asked Mr. Revson just that question. I told him that I was very pleased with my situation at ITT, where I ran a $5 billion operation, more than half of the corporation's business. That I was not a hotshot marketing man. That I was oriented in high technology—a business that was entirely different from

nity, particularly in the ethical or prescription drugs which did not depend heavily on consumer advertising expenditures, as Clairol did. As a result, he involved himself in the acquisition of Mead-Johnson & Co. and of Bristol Labs., his ethical pharmaceutical division. B-M's Bufferin is now running neck to neck with Sterling Drug Inc.'s Bayer Aspirin. As evidence of his competitiveness, Dick waged a tough advertising and marketing battle with McNeil Labs, a division of Johnson & Johnson, when the latter moved to make its Tylenol the top analgesic seller. Dick Gelb is having the time of his life.

Another story, but with a twist, is that of Michel Bergerac. Bilingual in French and English, bright, motivated, and charismatic, Michel joined the Cannon Electric Co. in 1957 as sales representative. He was 24. Cannon was an international supplier of telecommunication components for industrial, commercial, and military use, and young Michel, a high achiever from the start, advanced quickly up the ladder. Within five months he was made international representative, then international sales supervisor, then sales manager. By July 1961 he was VP and director of overseas operations. He was only 28, but he was just beginning to move.

On November 30, 1963, International Telephone and Telegraph Corp. bought Cannon for $33 million in stock, and three years later Michel Bergerac was promoted to group general manager. In quick succession he was named group GM and VP, ITT Europe, as well as VP of ITT itself, and in 1971 executive VP, ITT Europe. He did so well that in 1972 he was named ITT's president in

Europe. In two more years he was elected executive vice-president of the huge corporation. He was now 41 and still moving.

At that point the founder and boss man of Revlon, Charles Revson, came to Michel with an offer he could not refuse. Annual salary of $325,000 for five years, a $1.5 million bonus—just for beginning an employment contract—and an option on 70,000 shares of Revlon stock, potentially worth millions. A deal of deals. Michel Bergerac left ITT for the presidency of Revlon early in 1975, with Charlie Revson's promise that he'd succeed him as chairman and CEO when Charlie stepped down or died. If Charlie reneged, Michel could leave and upon leaving (or being fired) he would keep his bonus and at least two years' salary—almost $2.5 million for two years' work or less.

Actually, when he hired Michel under these fantastic terms, Charlie knew he was suffering from terminal cancer and had less than a year to live. Hugely successful as an entrepreneur, Revson had one managerial weakness. He had to do everything himself, or watch others closely to see that they did what he wanted and in his way, especially in marketing and advertising. Thus Revlon became a revolving door for a long line of able and famous executives, and as time passed Charlie Revson found it difficult to hire executives of talent and ambition. He was able to get Bergerac only because, in addition to a lavish financial and contractual arrangement, he made fairly clear that he would suceed Revson. And that is exactly what happened. Charlie Revson died on Au-

gust 24, 1975, at 68 years of age Michel Bergerac was named chief Revlon.

None of this would have hap Bergerac had ITT been unaware of his tial, or had it not given him the opport in headquarters. Interviewed in his off ninth floor of New York's marble-faced Building, the tall, balding, mustached, tired Mr. Bergerac could not have been mo more willing to answer questions. His offi furnished and has a magnificent, breathtaki entire city.

"Why do some executives of merged cor ceed with headquarters?" I asked. As Mr. E swered, the accents of his schools, the Sor Cambridge, could be distinguished.

"They learn quickly and they are able to needs to be done—with ease and éclat. Instead ing of themselves, what is good for them, exec merged companies who succeed with headquart out what is good for the corporation and proceed just that—take the needed steps to improve the co tion's well-being. If what is good for the corporatio happens to be good for them, then the end resul happy marriage."

Asked for some other qualities and motivations help an executive of a merged company with headqu ters, Mr. Bergerac smiled and said, "There is no r secret. In the first place, he must continue his loyalty

that of Revlon. 'So why pick on me?' I asked. Mr. Revson looked me straight in the eye and said: 'But you know how to make money.' "

But there were other reasons for the choice. It was Michel's knowledge of the international market, his charisma, style, and ability to work with other executives. All that he had learned and applied at ITT.

"Charlie Revson never patted his executives on the back, even when their achievements were monumental," I commented. "Will you?"

"I am not sure whether I will do more back patting than Mr. Revson did. But it will not be necessary. The operational structure we have set up now will make it possible for each of our managers to know whether he is succeeding or failing and to what extent."

"How is that? What are you doing for your executives that had not been done before?"

"It is not money, as has been reported in some quarters. I am not paying them any more, although they are well compensated. What they are getting now is information which they did not receive before. They are receiving information of the kind that will help them to do their job effectively. At all times, from here on, they will see the total picture—from marketing to production to budgeting. In this way, and at last, they are and will be able to face the realities of their executive life. With this meaningful type of information they now also have full authority to run their specific operations. And as a result, they now have a greater opportunity for self-fulfillment."

My final question: "In your opinion and based on

your experience, what are the keys to a successful merger?" His answer:

"First come the financials. They must be correct and they must not dilute the stock of the acquiring corporation. Then, the corporation buying a company wants to make sure that it has a most able and productive management team. And finally, there must be some assurance that this management group will be willing to remain on the job—and grow."

I followed Mr. Bergerac's activities after Mr. Revson died. He was putting into effect his own style of management, I found, and it was working exceptionally well. Although he delegated authority to every department for almost every function, he watched budgets and expenses himself very carefully. As a result, in the first year of his direction, Revlon wound up with sales of $750 million, a gain of almost 20 percent, and profits in excess of $62 million, an increase of more than 15 percent. He did even better in 1976. His goal was a billion-dollar corporation with profits exceeding $100 million, and in 1977 it seemed he could do it.

As the second largest (Avon is first) cosmetic company, Revlon's potential is limited only by the industry itself. Accordingly, it plans to expand by mergers and acquisitions as well as by growing in areas besides cosmetics. Product lines in, and new marketing approaches for, the company's pharmaceutical division are already under development. Personally experienced in acquisitions, Mr. Bergerac, during his tenure at ITT, directed the addition of more than a hundred companies during three years, increasing his division sales by $2.2 billion to $5 billion, as noted. Now, with less than 15 percent of the total cosmetics and fragrance market, Mr. Bergerac is aiming for 20 percent or better. He believes he can do it with new products and updated marketing, and by strengthening the organization's total structure. Emphasis from here on will also be placed on planning and communications. The company operates in seven profit centers, each aimed at specific market segments, and each with its own management, production line, and store space program. Most important, his units are communicating with one another, quite a difference from the way Mr. Revson ran the business. Mr. Bergerac himself is now making house calls on stores to see how his products are displayed and sold, and to exchange ideas with merchandising executives at the retail level. There is little doubt that Mr. Bergerac's experience with ITT, especially at the international level, helps him operate a new and greater Revlon.

As difficult and pressure-packed as it may be to work for Harold Geneen and the $12 billion ITT, Michel Bergerac is not an isolated example of people who made it there. Look at what happened to Arthur T. Woerthwein.

Arthur was executive vice-president and a substantial stockholder of Bell & Gossett, the $40 million pump and valve firm, when it merged with ITT in 1963. During the first year thereafter, Art remained where he was, giving Harold Geneen and his associates an opportunity to observe him in action. Harold liked what he saw and Art began to move up in the corporate hierarchy—but fast.

By 1966 he was elected a corporate vice-president, and soon was named group executive for ITT's Technical and Industrial Products Group. With 1975 sales exceeding $350 million it was one of the corporation's most profitable units, a substantial and growing business in itself. Still in his fifties, Arthur Woerthwein looks forward to more personal and corporate growth.

What made it possible for him to make it with headquarters? Mr. Woerthwein, friendly and personable, replied: "Understanding the business." Why do so many executives fail? "They do not seem to be able to tell their people to do what is needed to be done."

Take it from one who succeeded admirably: Know the business well and direct your operating staffs so they too will have the bottom line in mind. Arthur knows this personally. In the first place, he is oriented to and experienced in finance like the big man himself, Harold Geneen. And nothing—just nothing—impresses the CEO of a large public corporation more than a man who can improve profitability. Second, Arthur Woerthwein was helped and encouraged by his predecessor, John T. Lobb. Lobb, who knew the ITT ropes and proved a good teacher, is now head of Northern Electric Co., Ltd., Canada's largest utility company.

Asked for advice on surviving and growing in large public corporations, Mr. Woerthwein said: "Understanding numbers is absolutely vital. Additionally, the executive, especially the president, of the company merging with a large public corporation should make no promises relating to sales, profits, and growth potential to be ex-

gust 24, 1975, at 68 years of age. Shortly thereafter Michel Bergerac was named chief executive officer of Revlon.

None of this would have happened to Michel Bergerac had ITT been unaware of his managerial potential, or had it not given him the opportunity to move up in headquarters. Interviewed in his office on the forty-ninth floor of New York's marble-faced General Motors Building, the tall, balding, mustached, handsomely attired Mr. Bergerac could not have been more relaxed, nor more willing to answer questions. His office is elegantly furnished and has a magnificent, breathtaking view of the entire city.

"Why do some executives of merged companies succeed with headquarters?" I asked. As Mr. Bergerac answered, the accents of his schools, the Sorbonne and Cambridge, could be distinguished.

"They learn quickly and they are able to do what needs to be done—with ease and éclat. Instead of thinking of themselves, what is good for them, executives of merged companies who succeed with headquarters find out what is good for the corporation and proceed to do just that—take the needed steps to improve the corporation's well-being. If what is good for the corporation also happens to be good for them, then the end result is a happy marriage."

Asked for some other qualities and motivations that help an executive of a merged company with headquarters, Mr. Bergerac smiled and said, "There is no real secret. In the first place, he must continue his loyalty to the company merged into the corporation and he should try to be flexible enough to be able to adjust to the needs of his new environment."

I then commented: "About 30 years ago Bud Schulberg wrote a novel called *What Makes Sammy Run?* Sammy, the character, personified the upcoming, pushy, 'let-no-one-stand-in-my-way' business executive of that time. How would you describe today's upcoming professional business executive?" His answer: "He is the very opposite, 180 degrees removed, from the type of a manager described in *What Makes Sammy Run?*"

"Why do most executives of private companies in a merger situation fail?"

"They are more concerned with themselves than the needs of the corporation. And they do not learn quickly enough. They do not do their homework well," he replied.

I changed the subject. "Charlie Revson hired so many able executives and then fired them. The Revlon executive suite, expensively but attractively carpeted and furnished and surrounded by beautiful and elegant secretaries, turned out to be the proverbial revolving door. Thus, he never really selected a successor to himself until your appointment. Why did he pick you?"

He smiled. "As a matter of fact, I asked Mr. Revson just that question. I told him that I was very pleased with my situation at ITT, where I ran a $5 billion operation, more than half of the corporation's business. That I was not a hotshot marketing man. That I was oriented in high technology—a business that was entirely different from

Europe. In two more years he was elected executive vice-president of the huge corporation. He was now 41 and still moving.

At that point the founder and boss man of Revlon, Charles Revson, came to Michel with an offer he could not refuse. Annual salary of $325,000 for five years, a $1.5 million bonus—just for beginning an employment contract—and an option on 70,000 shares of Revlon stock, potentially worth millions. A deal of deals. Michel Bergerac left ITT for the presidency of Revlon early in 1975, with Charlie Revson's promise that he'd succeed him as chairman and CEO when Charlie stepped down or died. If Charlie reneged, Michel could leave and upon leaving (or being fired) he would keep his bonus and at least two years' salary—almost $2.5 million for two years' work or less.

Actually, when he hired Michel under these fantastic terms, Charlie knew he was suffering from terminal cancer and had less than a year to live. Hugely successful as an entrepreneur, Revson had one managerial weakness. He had to do everything himself, or watch others closely to see that they did what he wanted and in his way, especially in marketing and advertising. Thus Revlon became a revolving door for a long line of able and famous executives, and as time passed Charlie Revson found it difficult to hire executives of talent and ambition. He was able to get Bergerac only because, in addition to a lavish financial and contractual arrangement, he made fairly clear that he would suceed Revson. And that is exactly what happened. Charlie Revson died on Au-

nity, particularly in the ethical or prescription drugs which did not depend heavily on consumer advertising expenditures, as Clairol did. As a result, he involved himself in the acquisition of Mead-Johnson & Co. and of Bristol Labs., his ethical pharmaceutical division. B-M's Bufferin is now running neck to neck with Sterling Drug Inc.'s Bayer Aspirin. As evidence of his competitiveness, Dick waged a tough advertising and marketing battle with McNeil Labs, a division of Johnson & Johnson, when the latter moved to make its Tylenol the top analgesic seller. Dick Gelb is having the time of his life.

Another story, but with a twist, is that of Michel Bergerac. Bilingual in French and English, bright, motivated, and charismatic, Michel joined the Cannon Electric Co. in 1957 as sales representative. He was 24. Cannon was an international supplier of telecommunication components for industrial, commercial, and military use, and young Michel, a high achiever from the start, advanced quickly up the ladder. Within five months he was made international representative, then international sales supervisor, then sales manager. By July 1961 he was VP and director of overseas operations. He was only 28, but he was just beginning to move.

On November 30, 1963, International Telephone and Telegraph Corp. bought Cannon for $33 million in stock, and three years later Michel Bergerac was promoted to group general manager. In quick succession he was named group GM and VP, ITT Europe, as well as VP of ITT itself, and in 1971 executive VP, ITT Europe. He did so well that in 1972 he was named ITT's president in

pected after the merger that he will not be able to deliver." He added:

"The rewards for the independent entrepreneur in a merger situation with a corporation such as ITT are great. But he must learn to adjust to the corporate structure and he must make sure that the promises he made before the merger will materialize after the merger. If he cannot do both and if he does not understand numbers, then the executive will be in trouble."

It was obvious to me that Mr. Woerthwein likes Harold Geneen and admires him as a human being. Mr. Geneen is a creative executive, he said, unusual for a numbers-oriented person, and "he is always able to give new ideas, loads of them, to executives of companies that ITT acquires—more than they can develop themselves—and he is always ready to help."

Mr. Woerthwein pointed out that his associates in the old Bell & Gossett company (now ITT Bell & Gossett Hydronics) also did well with ITT. R. Edwin Moore, chairman of B&G, remained until retirement in 1974, President W. A. Boone until he retired in 1975.

Let's take another case.

In the fall of 1965, Corn Products (now CPC International Inc.) acquired Ott Chemical Co., a small industrial chemicals firm of Muskegon, Michigan. Dr. James R. Eiszner was Ott's executive vice-president and chief operating officer. Already embarked on an expansion program, Corn Products bought Ott for two major reasons. First, it wanted to explore the industrial chemicals field. Second, it was impressed by the young chemist-administrator. Dr. Eiszner, it felt, could prove valuable in its own development and growth program.

Within a few years, the second reason was more compelling than the first. Having seen his managerial capabilities in action, Corn Products named Eiszner president of Ott in 1967 and in 1969 chairman of the board and chief executive officer. He then held executive positions with CPC's Development and Industrial divisions until 1971, when he was named president of CPC International's Industrial Division and elected a corporate VP. In 1975, he was elected a CPC director.

In the fall of 1972, however, CPC sold substantially all of the Ott assets to the Story Chemical Corp., Athens, Georgia. Although Ott manufactured a variety of intermediate chemicals for the agricultural-chemical and pharmaceutical industries, CPC felt it was not right for its overall program. Instead it decided to expand its chemical business with its S. B. Penick & Co., a highly successful acquisition that manufactured bulk medicinal and industrial fine chemicals, antibiotics, pest control chemicals, and botanical products. Shy, low key, studious, with a thorough knowledge of his field, Dr. Eiszner ran a business that represented 48 percent of CPC International's $2.7 billion dollar operation. Although Ott was gone, Eiszner remained and on January 1, 1977, he moved another step higher on the ladder to executive vice-president and chief administrative officer, just below President and CEO James W. McKee, Jr. With CPC's total volume pushing $3 billion, it is clear Eiszner has made it big with CPC headquarters.

Nabisco, Inc., New York, is the nation's largest biscuit and cracker company. With 1976 sales of more than $2 billion and net earnings of $77 million, it has diversified almost entirely through acquisition. For some time a multinational operation, Nabisco is also in such fields as snack foods, cereals, pet foods, pharmaceuticals and toiletries, hobbies, toys and table games, household furnishings, food services, frozen foods, and candy. Sure, it has had its share of merger failures, but more of them succeeded. Still, very few presidents and other top people Nabisco acquired ever made it big with headquarters. One notable exception, however, is Jim Welch, Jr. of the James O. Welch Co., Cambridge, Massachusetts.

Jim Welch, Sr. started his candy business in the twenties. He made fudge in his kitchen and sold it himself, wholesaler to wholesaler, and in some instances from store to store. Surviving the thirties and growing in the forties, by the late fifties and early sixties his company was one of the largest and most profitable in the industry. With no dearth of suitors, he sold to Nabisco in 1963 for $12 million in stock, becoming its largest individual shareholder. Elected a director of Nabisco (a position he still actively holds), he left Nabisco after only a short time, preferring to devote himself to community and charitable organizations. He also wanted to serve on other boards and take care of his various investments. His son, a vice-president before the merger, launched on a new and bigger career with Nabisco. Under his direction the Nabisco candy division became one of the largest confectionery units in the industry. Its line has been refined, new products introduced, and markets expanded. Whether the quiet, unassuming, well-organized and able Jim Jr. would have met the same success had the elder Welch continued to operate an independent company is hard to guess. We can tell that young Jim has fit into the vast Nabisco hierarchy as a good, professional manager can and should. After several moves up the corporate ladder, in 1976, at age 45, he was promoted to the presidency of SPD (Specialty Products Division), which accounts for just about every line of products Nabisco makes and markets except biscuits and crackers.

Easily a most notable success story, and for a very special reason, in the merger field is that of Matthew B. Rosenhaus. His J. B. Williams Co., widely known manufacturer and marketer of pharmaceuticals and toiletries, was acquired by Nabisco in 1971, marking the entrance of this special and volatile field by the conservative and largest biscuit, cracker manufacturer. It was also the highest price up to that time—$60 million of its stock—that Nabisco had paid for a company. Williams is known for its Geritol brand of vitamins and minerals, Sominex sleep aid, Aqua Velva aftershave lotion, and other proprietary medicinals and toiletries. A number of unexpected postmerger problems developed in this acquisition, largely because the Williams products and operational and marketing methods and approaches differed considerably, especially in its very hard hitting advertising program, from those of Nabisco. However, basics were eventually straightened out and today Williams is an important profit producer for Nabisco with considerable growth potential. Mr. Rosenhaus, one of Nabisco's biggest stockholders, has done well with the parent company, bringing much strength and executive expertise as vice-chairman to the board of directors of Nabisco, and continuing as CEO of Williams.

The H. J. Heinz Co. has other good cases of making it with headquarters. One with a particularly interesting angle is that of Anthony J. F. (Tony) O'Reilly, a management wunderkind of the past decade.

A brilliant Irishman with a great sense of humor, Tony was managing director of the Irish Sugar Company, Ltd., Dublin, and Erin Food Ltd., its subsidiary, both owned by the Irish government. Heinz acquired neither company, but it did agree in 1967 to form Heinz-Erin Ltd., a sales and marketing operation, to distribute certain products in the United Kingdom through Heinz's British sales force. Tony was doing a tremendous job for ISC and Heinz knew it. In 1969, at age 33, Tony was appointed managing director of H. J. Heinz Co. of Canada Ltd., the corporation's largest international operation. Three years later he was named senior vice-president–Europe, and in quick succession became executive VP and CEO of the entire H. J. Heinz Co. He is, of course, a member of the Heinz board and a substantial shareholder, and it will surprise no one if he soon becomes CEO.

The interesting thing is, until only recently Tony worked just part of the time for Heinz, commuting from Pittsburgh to Dublin each week to look after his personal, substantial business interests there. But then, almost from the beginning of his association with the company, Heinz felt that Tony O'Reilly could do more for them on a part-time basis than another professional manager could full time. It proves that the time you put into your business is not necessarily the key to success with headquarters. Accomplishment is what counts.

John Bryan, Jr.'s promotion to the presidency of Consolidated Foods in Chicago has things in common with Michel Bergerac's rise. Consolidated, like Revlon, had a crusty, brilliant, hard-hitting but difficult entrepreneur at its helm, and like the late Charles Revson, Nate Cummings built a $2.5 billion conglomerate the hard way—with little money but plenty of guts, management creativity, and hard work. Whereas Charlie Revson is dead, however, the 78-year-old Nate is very much alive, still pushing hard and still trying to control the company (as honorary chairman) that he built in his image. The difference between Bryan and Bergerac is that 34-year-old Jack Bryan got to the top from the presidency of his family company, the Bryan Packing Co., Inc., a $160 million Mississippi meat packing operation, which Consolidated bought in 1968.

John H. Bryan, Jr. was born the day that his father launched a small slaughtering and meat packing plant next door to the family home in the small town of West Point, Mississippi. Like other self-made, hard-driving entrepreneurs, Jack's father expected his son to follow in his footsteps, but young Jack had no interest in working for this bossy, strong-willed, dominating man. As a matter of fact, after graduating from Memphis, Tennessee's

Southwestern College with a degree in economics, he told his father in no uncertain terms that he would not join the family business. Instead, he continued his education in economics and business management at the University of Virginia and received an MBA at Mississippi State University—whereupon Jack and his father went through an interesting change. Jack decided he would join the family company, and his father insisted that his son replace him as president. The elder Bryan left, putting the company totally into Jack's hands, and began dabbling, with great success, in other business enterprises. For Dad, the decision was a masterstroke. Totally on his own and working long hours, the young president and CEO embarked on a vigorous expansion. When done he had increased sales from $18 million to $160 million a year.

At this time, Consolidated called on him. The big conglomerate had problems; profits were clearly on the decline. Jack Bryan made plain that if he took the job he would have full and complete operating power—not Nate Cummings. He set an almost around-the-clock schedule for himself and began to make organizational changes from the start. He sold off an unprofitable furniture operation, reorganized the corporation's toy and home furnishing divisions, and introduced tougher management and budgetary controls. (He also moved to sell its Fuller Brush subsidiary but, perhaps fortunately, he didn't. In the mid-seventies it was becoming profitable again.) Bryan changed the mix of Consolidated's board by adding five "outsiders," including economist Paul W.

McCracken, former chairman of the President's Council of Economic Advisors, increasing the board from 15 to 20 and giving the outsiders numerical superiority.

The point is, Jack Bryan made it with Consolidated Foods because he's professionally trained and had entrepreneurial experience. If Nate Cummings is abrasive and hard on his executives, Jack is deliberate, calm, and friendly. It also goes to show there is absolutely no pattern in making it with headquarters. Some do it one way, others in different ways, and the executive of a merged operation who wants to reach the top has to find his own.

Take George W. Blackwood. A young chemist just out of Harvard in 1937, George had difficulty finding a job when he came upon Bradley Dewey, Charles Almy, and their young chemical company in Cambridge, Massachusetts. Both were Harvard chemists too, and both had degrees from MIT. They were impressed with George, but the only job they could offer him was laboratory assistant. He took it. By the time Dewey and Almy merged into W. R. Grace & Co. in December 1954, George Blackwood was vice-president and sales manager, and Dewey & Almy had grown from a $4 million to a $35 million dollar company. In two years, Mr. Blackwood was president of the Dewey & Almy Chemical Division of Grace. In 1966 he was elected a group vice-president and was named group executive of its newly formed Industrial Chemicals Group, which included Dewey & Almy and other Grace specialty chemical operations, but was different from its present Industrial Chemicals Group. By the time Mr. Blackwood completed his assignment and received a further promotion, the equivalent operation of the old Dewey & Almy business and what grew out of it reached sales approaching $1 billion a year. In 1967, a time of depression for the agricultural chemicals business, Mr. Blackwood was named group executive of Grace's Agricultural Chemicals Group. He did so well here that promotions followed. By 1976 he was elected executive vice-president for operations. Shortly after that he was named vice-chairman and chief operation officer of the corporation.

Explaining his success, he said, "I was fortunate in having had fortuitous training. Bradley Dewey aimed at perfection in management while Charles Almy proved to be a great teacher."

Today, Grace's Agricultural Chemicals Group, with sales of $350 million, is one of the most profitable in the corporation and one of the largest in the industry, but as its one-time executive vice-president for operations, George was without a profit center. What did he do? "Find problems and try to solve them." Since he was the first Grace EVP to have this special assignment, I asked whether Grace people brought their problems to him. His answer: "At first they were afraid of me. But as time went on they did indeed come in with their problems and it proved to be real fun trying to help them."

Now vice-chairman and CEO of a diversified corporation pushing toward annual sales of $4 billion, what advice would he give young executives wanting to grow with their new parent companies?

"Learn every facet of your business. If you happen to be expert in sales, then learn all you can about production and finance. If you are a financial expert, learn all you can about sales, marketing, production, etc., etc. What an upcoming executive of a big corporation needs is a balance—a balance and knowledge of every phase of the business."

But why do so many executives in a merger fail?

"They are too set in their ways and/or unable to communicate; and in some cases entrepreneurial executives are so strong-willed that they feel they have exclusivity to ideas."

The unique thing about Donald R. Keough of The Coca-Cola Company is that he made it with headquarters not once but three times, reaching his present position as president of all the Americas (North, Central, and South) and senior vice-president of the Georgia parent company in three interesting stages.

In the food business since 1950, Don is Iowa born and bred and a 1949 graduate of Creighton University with a B.S. degree. After a brief, invigorating stint in broadcasting, he joined product jobber Paxton & Gallagher in August 1950, teaching part time as well in the University's Industrial Relations and Business Administration Schools. At Paxton & Gallagher, headquartered in Omaha, his first job was assistant advertising manager.

Although Paxton & Gallagher distributed and wholesaled almost every conceivable product from hardware to candy, it also owned and distributed Butter-Nut coffee throughout its Nebraska to California territory. When Paxton & Gallagher was acquired in 1959 by Gilbert and Clarke Swanson, famous for Swanson frozen foods (subsequently sold to the Campbell Soup Company), Don went to Swanson as marketing director. The Swansons changed P&G to Butter-Nut Foods Co., expanding its coffee business throughout the West, but selling the old-line jobbing enterprise. Coffee continued as its principal product, but other specialty foods were added, until in 1961 Swanson sold Butter-Nut to Duncan Foods Co., Houston, Texas. Don became marketing vice-president of the combined operation in the United States. In 1964 Duncan Foods Co. was itself sold to The Coca-Cola Company, remaining intact until 1967 when Coca-Cola formed its Foods Division. Among its products were Duncan's coffee and tea, to which it added citrus and fruit drinks.

Don? He became vice-president and director of marketing for all products. From there moving up to senior vice-president, in 1971 he was elected president of the Foods Division and a vice-president of The Coca-Cola Company. Two years later he was named executive vice-president of Coca-Cola USA and in May 1974 he was elected president of Coca-Cola USA, plus senior vice-president of The Coca-Cola Company. Don was only in his upper forties.

Quite a step up for an assistant advertising manager of a regional jobbing company. Still, it did take him 20 years and three major leaps, but maybe that was part of the fun. How did he do it? A few things he told me in 1975 reveal a lot:

"Never for one moment have I worried about the next job."

"Coke and its people have touched every phase of my life."

"Understanding the essence of the business—to look outward with joy and excitement in the marketplace are key elements in the success of an executive of a merged company with headquarters."

"Selling—salesmanship—represents the biggest word in business."

Talking with Don Keough is a delightful but dizzying experience. He is a natural storyteller, loves business and business people, and loves talking about it. Obviously the seven hundred franchised Coca-Cola bottlers in the United States and the many others in the rest of the Americas look forward to a visit from him and he visits dozens of them every year, meeting many more at conventions and sales conferences. He is also a listener, keenly interested in people and what makes them tick, always ready to help with ideas and practical suggestions, but he is foremost an active, creative doer.

Thus, through natural inclination, training, and experience, Don Keough has all of the basic talents to succeed with headquarters. But he has also had two other vital things going for him: the good fortune of knowing and working with senior executives who are interested in giving other people a chance to grow, and a wife with sensitivity and judgment who is not afraid to express her feelings.

Here is some more of Don's sage advice for anyone

who hopes to succeed with the people at headquarters:

"He must be willing to transfer his loyalty from the merged to the acquiring company. Totally and without reservation. And his loyalty must be explicit to the company rather than to an individual in that company."

"There is no steady climb upward . . . there can be plenty of plateaus . . . but if one is to succeed, he cannot stop at plateaus."

"There is a price to pay in moving upward. People forget that in a merger situation it is necessary to make sacrifices, some that could be very difficult. The executive who wishes to move up must be willing and ready to do what the company asks of him. And it is helpful if one can anticipate what the company will want and need rather than wait to be asked or told."

Now hear what Norton Simon's David Mahoney says.

Asked the same basic question, David looked at me as though it had never occurred to him. After a few seconds of silence:

"I don't know. I really don't have a quick, definitive answer to your question. . . ."

A strange reply from one of the nation's most successful, verbal, sophisticated, and civilized professional managers—an entrepreneur who made it very big indeed. Handsome, friendly, quick-witted, a fast-talking Bronx-born Irishman, Dave launched his own advertising business at 28 with a $10,000 bank loan after resigning a $25,000 post with one of the country's largest, most noteworthy agencies where his future seemed secure.

Now chairman and chief executive officer of the $2 billion conglomerate, Dave Mahoney never lost his entrepreneurial spirit.

"What are the special qualities that make it possible for an executive to make it big with a public corporation?" he repeated. At first slowly and deliberately, then rattling like a machine gun:

"What special qualities? Special is the word. Panache. Verve. Guts, judgment, style, flair. What makes a great quarterback? I don't really know. I doubt whether anyone can put his finger on it. Not even the coach himself. There are a lot of good, well-coached quarterbacks. And before each game, almost always before each important play, the coach signals to the quarterback what precise play—previously carefully rehearsed—to take. Then signals are called and presto, the quarterback calls for an entirely different play. What compulsion, what thought, what idea made him pick that particular play, which in turn was the right one since the needed yardage was gained and a little more besides? No one really knows, perhaps not even the quarterback himself. It is that something special, that indescribable quality that makes a great quarterback.

"Why are you the good writer that you are? What makes a great painter? A superior designer? The superb trial lawyer? The star quality of an actor? It is a special combination of dynamics. And a lot more besides. That is why some make it and others do not."

David Mahoney, at 52, has all the qualities of a superb executive. He is dynamic, he dominates. He takes

over, but is likable. He has that great quality of getting
along with people, and the greater quality of attracting
people who want to help him. Let's look at his career
more closely.

Selling his advertising agency for $500,000 after five
years, he accepted an offer of a client, the Good Humor
Corp., to sign on as president. That was in 1956, when
he was 33. He did a tremendous job, guiding this specialty ice cream manufacturer and marketer to an impres-
sive record before it was acquired by Thomas J. Lipton,
Inc., in 1961. His next move was to Colgate-Palmolive as
executive vice-president, the Number 2 man in a company with almost a billion dollars in annual volume. He
remained there five years, compiling a record of accomplishment, especially in the firm's domestic product
marketing area, then left. He wanted to run his own
company again and it appeared that his boss at Colgate
would be around for a long time.

Next came the presidency and top spot with Canada
Dry Corp., in which Norton Simon and his Hunt Foods
& Industries, Inc. held a strong stock position with op-
tions for more. Despite the Canada Dry name, it was a
floundering operation when in 1966, at 43, David
Mahoney took on the challenge. That was the year I first
met him, at the annual convention of the soft drink in-
dustry. Canada Dry threw a lavish cocktail party in one
of the grand ballrooms of Houston's grand hotel, the
Warwick. When the room was about half filled with
Canada Dry bottlers and other industry people, David
Mahoney entered. We felt it immediately. He was new

to soft drinks and acquainted with only a handful of people there—mostly his own executives—but it did not matter. He was a great mixer (sorry about that) and he mixed as he never had before, or maybe as he always did at such functions. Within minutes the center of attention, he was calling many in the room by their first name. He didn't linger with anyone, however, but moved from one group to another, greeting newcomers with a smile and friendly bearing.

David proved a huge success at Canada Dry. By 1975 it accounted for $333 million in sales and more than $31 million in profit before taxes. Norton Simon, president of Hunt Foods & Industries, Inc., had been buying into Canada Dry for some time and now had a big stake in it. Looking for a new chief executive officer to increase its profitability before buying a controlling interest, he had selected David Mahoney because "he had been successful in running his own business." Simon also liked David's varied experience and "his high degree of human sensitivity and compassion."

Anyway, David Mahoney did so well with Canada Dry, which before long did come under Norton Simon's control, that a strong bond of friendship and admiration developed between the two men. When Simon formed Norton Simon, Inc. with Hunt Foods, The McCall Pattern Co., and Canada Dry, about two years later, David became his president and chief operating officer. That was in 1968. Less than a year later, in the summer of 1969, David Mahoney reached the top. He became Norton Simon's chief executive officer.

David Mahoney now runs a hard-hitting, well-managed, growing, diversified public corporation with nearly $2 billion in annual sales and net profit after taxes of $82.7 million. His own annual earnings are in the neighborhood of half a million dollars and his net worth, including his Norton Simon, Inc. stock, is approximately $20 million. The corporation consists of six major profit centers—Food and Food Service, Cosmetics & Fashion, Soft Drinks, Distilled Spirits, Packaging, and the Number 2 car renter, Avis, Inc. Mahoney's present thrust is in cosmetics and fashion. About a year or so ago, he acquired Halston Enterprises, Inc., the organization headed by one of the country's leading fashion designers. (He uses only his family name and even David, with his superb memory, had to think hard to remember his given name: Roy.) Using the Halston name and talents, Norton Simon, Inc., is expanding from wearing apparel to fragrances and, by licensing agreements, into luggage and related products. If anything, he expects his acquisition activity to intensify.

What does he look for in buying new companies?

"Fit, commitment, and vision." By fit he means that the corporation and its product mix must match, and develop with, Norton Simon's. By commitment he means to growth. By vision? "We are interested in a company whose management has the vision needed for creative building that operates in areas that excite consumer interest and need. What we are doing with Halston is a good case in point. Another important consideration in our acquisition program is redeployment potential of the assets of the company we want to buy. As well as the potential of the effective utilization of management."

Not everything he acquired (or inherited) is still part of NSI. Again the matter of fit. Some acquisitions didn't fit, or no longer did as the corporation and times changed. Said Chairman Mahoney:

"A significant aspect of our operating progress was the substantial completion of our asset redeployment program, which included the sale of the Redbook Publishing Co., the McCall printing plant in Dayton, the Denver Chemical Mfg. Co., Talent Associates, Ltd., and the McCall Information Services Co., and the closing of the McCall printing plant at Glenn Dale, Maryland (accomplished through 1974–1975), and earlier the sale of *McCall's* magazine.

"In support of our program to move from capital-intensive to marketing-intensive activities, we have (since 1968) redeployed a total of $426 million of net assets into consumer product business. As a result, today our consumer product operations account for 89 percent of sales and 83 percent of profits before taxes, compared with 64 percent and 70 percent respectively."

Obviously, therefore, if an executive of a merged company is to grow and become part of his new corporate management, he needs genuine managerial talent. He also needs thorough knowledge of the business. It also helps if he is personable but tough. He needs that special big corporation touch, a way to deal properly not only with his superiors and associates, but also with his employees. He must be aggressive but not pushy. Simply stated, if he is an exceptional person he will go far. Race, religion, ethnic background no longer matter. What really counts is ability, stamina, and creativity.

Look again at Beatrice Foods, a company that has obtained excellent managers through acquisitions and then promoted them within the corporation. At least a dozen of Beatrice Foods's top executives—executive vice-presidents and division presidents—joined this successful corporation as officers of acquired firms. In fact, the main reason that Beatrice grows so successfully is its emphasis on people and teamwork, according to Don L. Grantham, its recently retired president and chief operating officer. It's a management concept dating back to the time the company was first incorporated, 1898. What does it look for in its acquisitions and people? Said Mr. Grantham: "(1) Do we want this business? Does it fit? Do we have a home for it? (2) What has been the growth pattern over the years? In sales? In earnings? What is the future growth potential? (3) What is the quality of management? What is the depth?"

"The last point is the most important of all," Mr. Grantham noted. "The present management must be willing to stay with the company. These management people must be Beatrice Foods type people. People who can motivate others, get along with people, and they should have entrepreneurial spirit."

Beatrice Foods deems the people element so vital that it will not acquire a company unless it has a strong management team, willing and able to manage it for years with only normal supervision from the home office. By experience it knows the approach works. The staff at Beatrice Foods's headquarters is one of the smallest among all major corporations. Although the headquarters team stays in touch with the heads of the operating divisions and remains ready to provide needed services, it is the divisional presidents who operate Beatrice's diversified businesses. Jim Weiss, elected executive vice-president in 1975, is one of them.

Jim is a friend of long standing. No man to waste time, he gets to the crux of a question (and a business situation) quickly and with aplomb. What does he think is the key to success for the independent entrepreneurs who joined Beatrice Foods with their companies? Said Jim:

"The bottom line, the end result, is the basic determining factor from a long-range point of view, but it is not the only element of success for the formerly independent entrepreneur who merges his company with a large, listed public corporation.

"In my opinion and from my own experience, the human element—the relationship between people—is a primary factor," he continued. "While a corporation deals in products and services—and the successful production and marketing of such products and services determines profitability—people, human beings, comprise the corporate entity. Without people—good people, able, highly motivated people—there can be no business, nor corporation, large or small.

"The healthy, friendly but pragmatic interrelationship between the independent entrepreneur and his executive team, with whom he works on a regular basis, is a key to success. This team could include the person or persons to whom the divisional manager or president reports, the members of senior management at the local operating unit, as well as corporate level management."

Even in the budgeting process, people play a part. In presenting the annual budget for his divisions, Mr. Weiss deals with (1) people planning, (2) sales planning, (3) earnings planning, (4) new product planning, and (5) capital needs planning—and in that order. Asked what he means by "people planning," he replied:

"By 'people planning' I am referring to the present and future people who manage the various activities of the company, including middle management. The question that I ask is who is doing what today and who will be doing those things in the future? Who will be doing the creating of new products? Who will be doing the capital investment analysis? Who the production line direction and operation? The marketing? Who selling? And in every phase of the operation of the division and its satellites? Who will do the managing? Who will be the backup for whom? Who will deserve what promotion?"

So important does he consider the people planning function that he reviews it quarterly. So do the other division presidents and group managers—a major reason why Beatrice Foods is successful in growing people as well as profits.

215

Chapter

10

What Happens
If You Flop

WHAT CAN YOU DO if your merger fails?

Let's say you couldn't play the merger game by the rules—or not by the rules your partner laid out. Maybe you just didn't do what was expected of you, or just couldn't measure up. Or, you were doing your job well, with sales and profits of your division rising rapidly, but your parent was doing badly, perhaps so badly it was verging on collapse. What do you do? You took stock for your business and now it is sliding downward and fast. How do you get out?

All this and more happens in mergers and acquisitions. Not only have independent entrepreneurs failed to run their divisions well, but just as often large public corporations on an acquiring binge have discovered that some of their acquisitions don't have the fit they expected, or proved to be total disasters. Thus, the large number of spin-offs during the past few years. More and more we find corporations disposing of firms that "did not work out." What are your options? Here are some of them.

1. Sell your stock if it's not dangerously down with little possibility of recovery. Pick up your chips and run.

2. If you have a long-term contract—five years or more with two or three yet to run—try to have the corporation buy it out. This is common. A corporation prefers to buy out of a dissatisfied (or, in its opinion, incompetent) division head or other major executive. You will not receive the full contract amount, but you may well come out with half or more. It will depend on how you negotiate and how much the corporation wants you out.

3. The corporation decides to spin off your division—yours plus your own later acquisitions. You have a contract. Your problem: to work out a desirable arrangement with the company buying you. If you happen to be an important executive with unusual expertise in one or more areas of the business, you may have an ace in the hole. Play it.

4. Or, in the case of a spin-off, you could also take the initiative and find a "friendly," compatible buyer. Try to get an option and time frame, then go to work. It could be good for you, your associates, and your later health and growth.

5. Why not try a buyback? If you are unhappy with your parents and they with you, a buyback is a distinct

possibility. Although often thick with roadblocks and difficulties, it can be accomplished. You may have to pay more than you got for your business initially, but often you'll recapture it for less.

That is what I did, as touched upon earlier: It was a difficult, complicated task and it took more than six months of intense activity plus a few sleepless nights. Still accomplish it I did, with great satisfaction and much success later.

It was early in 1970. The recession was beginning and money was tight—the worst time to try to buy back a business, almost any business, not to mention one with some problems. (Mine, I will say unabashedly, were due to the corporation.) Here's how it happened.

My business was Magazines For Industry, Inc. Publisher of eight fairly small business magazines, with annual sales of $2.5 million and modest profits, we had real growth potential when we sold to Cowles Communications, Inc., a $200 million public corporation. Boasting a solid ten years of expansion, Cowles wanted to complete its communications empire by entering the business magazine field. Me? I wanted to build a large business and professional magazine division, one with sales of $50 million and net profits of $8 million, largely through acquisitions. Cowles offered me the opportunity. I could use its stock, its credit, its banking connections—all of high standing—plus cash, if necessary, to accomplish it.

Negotiations started in March 1966 and the merger was completed by the end of November. My associates and I received about 135,000 Cowles shares, trading at

15⅞ when the deal was agreed upon and 13¾ at the closing. Since I owned about 80 percent of MFI's stock, I received 101,000 shares of Cowles. I was named president of the new Cowles Business and Professional Magazine Division, elected to the board of directors of Cowles Communications, Inc., and given a seven-year contract. I was now a millionaire—on paper. In addition to my salary, I received more than $50,000 in dividends a year. Not a bad deal. Most important, I was now able to do what I had wanted to do for more than a dozen years— build a large, substantial operation. I felt I had the ability and the excellent staff to do it.

Within two years it seemed I would. I was successful in buying two companies, one a notable medical magazine company, and the other a smaller business magazine operation. My division sales reached $12.5 million and profits before taxes, $2.5 million. A great start. Cowles management and the business and professional magazine fraternity thought so too. Moreover, I had a good list of other prospects in the business and professional magazine field, and I could now visualize my $50 million sales, $8 million profit goal within another three years. From there? No telling.

Now, when I joined my fortunes with Cowles, its *Look* magazine was "bigger than *Life*" and was contributing about $4 million to the corporation's earnings. *Family Circle* was also going strong, recording profits of $2 million a year. The television and radio stations and the daily newspapers were also OK. The price of Cowles stock began to move up, soon reaching $21 a share, and there was talk among Cowles executives and on Wall Street that before long this would be a $50 stock. I began to dream new dreams, visualizing the worth of my 101,000 shares in the neighborhood of $5 million.

But as an active and somewhat rebellious member of the Cowles board, I began to see funny things happening at our meetings. I would call it unbelievable ineptitude.

Suddenly, instead of contributing a $4 million pretax profit, *Look* began to show losses, soon going a whopping $4 million into the red. *Family Circle* was going red too; its loss soon reached $2 million. The book division turned out to be a real disaster. Nothing but losses upon losses, year after year. *Venture*, a travel magazine that had never made money, was showing larger losses. Then, disaster of disasters, Chairman Mike Cowles, a legend in newspapers and magazines, induced the corporation to launch a daily newspaper in the growing Suffolk County on New York's Long Island. It was to compete, somewhat, with *Newsday*, a successful daily tabloid covering Nassau County, which proceeded to expand into our Suffolk County turf. We, on the other hand, were a failure from the start. Within a year or so, *The Suffolk Sun*'s losses amounted to $15 million. Since Cowles's total working capital was only $35 million, this huge loss, together with our other losses, put the corporate exchequer in a real bind.

As a result, the price of Cowles stock started to slide. From a high of $21 it went to $15, to $13, to $10, and soon to $7 a share. I had wanted to sell at the $21 high, but as a member of the corporation's board of directors and thus an insider, I was restricted by SEC Rule No. 133. I finally disposed of 6,000 shares at an average of $20 a share. The 96,000 shares I had left were worth only $672,000, however, and there was good reason to believe they would soon be worth even less, a fraction of their original value when my total holdings approximated $1.5 million.

So there I am, sitting on the Cowles board and watching things fall apart. I become frustrated and discouraged. Eventually the darkened, bleak *Sun* was folded, but much too late to save Cowles Communications, Inc. I try to make what I believe are constructive suggestions but they are quickly shot down. Instead of meaningful discussions I hear pronouncements by the tall, chain-smoking, yet still dignified chairman. Then, at a special board meeting, comes word that the highly successful and profitable Puerto Rico daily newspaper, the *San Juan Star*, is being sold for $10 million to shore up the corporation's dwindling cash position. It's clear to me that this is a desperation move. Knowing what's happening with *Look*, *Family Circle*, and the book division, it's obvious to me that new cash won't last very long. It's also clear I had better buy back my division, or at least my original company.

On Wednesday morning, February 25, 1970, I meet with Marvin Whatmore, president and chief operating officer of Cowles, and make my offer. He is not particularly stunned and says he will call a meeting of the executive committee at an early date and advise me of the decision. Briefly, here is what happened next.

Within two weeks, Mr. Whatmore reported that the committee was willing to sell Magazines For Industry, Inc., including the small business magazine company I had acquired, but not the Modern Medicine group of publications. He explained, however, that it would be necessary to invite bids from other would-be buyers to avoid possible stockholder suits, and he invited me to make my own. At the same time he explained that he would get a reputable appraiser to put a value on MFI, as a way of measuring the company against the offers. This he did, and eventually we agreed upon $1.25 million, in line with the appraisal and several other bids. Of this, $750,000 would be paid in cash at the closing, the balance of $500,000 on an open-end quarterly payout of 10 percent of MFI's profits after taxes.

Now that I had a deal, the job was to find $750,000 cash in the terribly tight money market. I tried several venture capital firms, which meant endless presentations, and in the end they demanded more of the action than I was willing to give up. Under no circumstances would I buy back our business unless I got full control, or a minimum of 51 percent of our stock. I then tried investment bankers. Again, more meetings and more presentations, and again nothing. And all the time Cowles Communications was pushing me for action—it had other willing buyers—and I still had a business to run.

Finally, I hit upon an entirely new approach. I would invite several of our key executives to participate in the buyback to the extent of $250,000, then ask our commercial bank, the Irving Trust Co., for a $500,000 term loan.

It seemed a great idea but it took a lot of doing. I assigned the direct job of obtaining the $250,000 to Marvin Toben, then our executive vice-president and now president and my right hand in running MFI. Within a week, Marv had signed up fifteen key MFI executives to join in the buyback. Several invested $25,000 each, our basic unit; Marv invested $75,000; John B. Mulligan, publisher of several of our magazines, $50,000; and the rest amounts averaging $5,000.

With commitments for $250,000 in my hand I met with a senior vice-president of Irving Trust and explained what I had in mind. Again, it took a bit of doing but we did get the $500,000 term loan we needed, and in the end, despite further problems, we succeeded in the buyback, in fact, of a bigger operation than originally we had sold to Cowles. The date was Friday, September 4, 1970. It was a good Labor Day weekend that year for us all.

What happened to Cowles Communications, Inc., that charismatic corporation built almost entirely through acquisition? Following our buyback, Cowles sold *Family Circle*, the Modern Medicine group, the Florida newspapers, the Memphis TV station WREG, and just about everything else to The New York Times Company. It received 2.6 million Class A shares, with limited voting rights, or approximately 23 percent of all classes of Times common stock at a value, at time of sale, of $39 million. Because this turned out to be its principal holding, Cowles soon became a closed-end, nondiversified management investment company under the Investment Company Act of 1940, as amended. The only operating businesses it has now are WESH-TV, Daytona Beach-Orlando, and KCCI-TV, Des Moines. It no longer publishes any magazines or newspapers. And as maybe a final irony, instead of launching the disastrous *Suffolk Sun*, it could have bought *Newsday*.

Since then, Magazines For Industry, Inc. has grown substantially. In mid-1977 our annual volume exceeded $6 million and our profits have increased every year since 1971, setting records in 1975, 1976, and 1977. In 1973 we launched a new and unusual magazine, the *Journal of Legal Medicine*, the official organ of the American College of Legal Medicine. Our annual advertising billings for this periodical alone are about $1 million. What happened to our contingent liability of $500,000? We paid out approximately $50,000 in profits during the first two years after our separation from Cowles, settling the $450,000 balance in cash for $140,000—which meant that we had bought ourselves back for $940,000.

Our story shows two major things. First, one way to get out when the corporate bubble begins to burst is through a buyback. And second, even a charismatic public corporation, built almost entirely through acquisition and with real growth potential, can fall apart if its management fails.

The Bottom Line

OK, YOU HAVE MERGED (or shall we say sold to?) Mr. Big. What next? What is in store for you? How do you behave from here on? Let's try another scenario.

Against the advice of your associates and accountant, you took stock—all stock—rather than stock and cash or all cash. You did so because you felt that with cash your tax bite would have been bigger than you could handle at this time. Besides, the common stock you received for your controlling interest was clearly marketable. Of course, you've agreed not to sell any of it during the first year following the merger, but in the second year you can begin to, at the rate of one-third of your holdings per year. Not a bad contract, to be sure. The first year will pass very fast, yes?

One thing does bother you, however. What will your stock do that first year? Probably not much. The economy is now fairly stable and no recession is ex-

225

pected, at least for another year or two. Your investment, almost a lifetime of work, pressure, and no little struggle, seems substantial and sound. Besides, it's selling at 12 times earnings, not low but satisfactory for a company still growing, and it also pays dividends. Three percent of its present price, $30 a share, isn't too bad, but with 100,000 shares, your annual dividend of 90 cents a share comes to $90,000 yearly. Your attorney advised you, correctly, to establish a ten-year revocable trust on behalf of your two children for one-third of your stock, and you did. This means that each child has a dividend income of $15,000 a year and you and your wife, $60,000. With your salary of $100,000—unchanged over the past three years—your taxes increase substantially, but you have a few other investments and securities, acquired earlier, which should help. All told, really not bad. You're OK financially—but what about your lifestyle?

Your personal life may not change very much but your business life will—dramatically and perhaps not to your liking. You are 55, in fairly good health, now president of one among several divisions under Mr. Big's supervision, all told with sales exceeding $1 billion. You head up a moderately profitable unit in your division and report to a division executive vice-president. You have a five-year contract. By the time it expires you will be 60, with five years to go before mandatory retirement (ten under the new federal law). You understand that your situation from here on will be different from what it was in the two decades past, so you are more concerned about your first five years with the company, rather than the second five or ten preceding retirement. You are absolutely correct. The first five are the most critical years in your business life and will determine what happens in the second. What you'll do now, some of it irrevocable, puts you a little on edge. That's all right, too. Complacency is probably your worst enemy in these early post-merger years. Remember that your company was bought for at least three important reasons: to increase corporate sales and profits, to introduce a new product line or new market, and to infuse new management talent into the corporate hierarchy. If you don't do this, you and your associates could be in trouble. It won't take long to find out whether you will or not, certainly no more than two years. You, your associates, and your operation will be watched from the moment the honeymoon ends. You make it or else.

Or else what? A spin-off, sell-off, or divestiture—whatever you call it, it's the same thing. In the hotshot sixties, acquiring corporations were disinclined to sell companies that hadn't quite panned out. They tried to find other ways to deal with their lemons, and some of those ways proved costly. No longer is it easy to "absorb" or "hide" losses, however, which is why corporations have recently been doing so much divesting, spinning off, or selling. Today, they would rather take their lumps, sometimes large, than stick by an outfit with a sluggish bottom line. Let's look at a few revealing examples.

Marx Toys was one of the more famous and profitable toy companies when acquired by The Quaker Oats

Co., a pioneer in the cereal field, but under Quaker's ownership, Marx languished. Before long it contributed not profits but losses to this profit-oriented company. Thus, rather than continue supporting Marx, in 1975 Quaker took a loss write-off of almost $12 million.

International Industries, Inc., a wunderkind of the merger-mad sixties, bought almost everything in sight and paid dearly. By the mid-seventies it faced bankruptcy. To hold its hungry creditors at bay, it sold off a group of its education companies, its Orange Julius chain of snack eateries, and its classier Copper Penny restaurants—all for a whopping $25 million loss. It was more than this type of firm could stand, and in the end it went belly up.

FMC Corporation—machinery and chemicals—is a great corporation in many ways. Its overall record is good. It bought several companies that looked fine at the closing but eventually proved burdens. Its synthetic fiber division, once the famous and profitable Avisco, had sales in 1975 of $317 million but an after-tax loss of more than $17 million. What did FMC do? Sold to a group of FMC executives for $60 million, despite the division's book value of $120 million.

A corporation may sell an unprofitable acquisition to the highest bidder, but more often it will offer the former owners or current management a buyback. Cooper Laboratories, Inc. spun off its 8 in 1 Pet Products, Inc. to its former owner for $1 million in cash and future payout. Texstar Corp. sold American Excelsior to current management for $6.5 million, using the proceeds to reduce debt and increase working capital. Imperial Industries, Inc. disposed of its Regal Wood Products Unit to a group of officers.

A few more examples: When Colgate-Palmolive Co. found that the Bauer & Black surgical support hosiery line, part of its otherwise profitable Kendall division, did not measure up to its standards, Becton, Dickenson and Company bought it. The medical and surgical instrument firm believed it would do just fine. Crompton & Knowles Corporation found it advisable to sell its packaging machinery division, an important early acquisition. It did, to a successful entrepreneur in the packaging machinery field—Gerry Ziffer—who is making out nicely with Redington, Inc.'s line of cartoning and wrapping equipment. Borden, Inc., which over the years converted an almost all-dairy operation into chemicals and specialty foods, disposed of Aunt Jane's pickle packing business and its liquid cane sugar unit. The pickle packer was "nongrowth," it said, and liquid cane sugar out of line with its overall expansion.

Here is a particularly unusual story of sell-off and buyback. Masco Corporation, an innovative manufacturer of faucets and a variety of extruded metal products, realized that its $19 million 1976 acquisition of Royce Electronics, a producer and marketer of CB radios, was a mistake. The CB market had gotten extremely competitive, and with its standard of 20 percent pretax earnings margins, Masco saw no way to operate Royce profitably. Thus, it sold 51 percent back to Royce management for $2 million cash and a $10 million note due in one year. In

addition, Masco will receive 50 percent of Royce's earnings, up to $12 million, for the next six years. Masco
could well profit from the deal, and Royce management
seems glad to have its company back. Now, if Royce
exercises an option to buy back the remaining 49 percent
for $20 million, Masco could make a real killing.

The point of this recital is that sometimes a bleak
situation turns out bright, for the seller and buyer both.
It may not be the worst thing to happen to a divisional
manager, who sold, and sometimes it can be a lifesaver.

The darker side to all this is, of course, the "unfriendly" takeover. There's been a spate of them lately
and they're not fun.

Say you sell your firm to a multimillion- or multibillion-dollar growth operation expecting everything to
be roses in years ahead. What happens? Your excellent
corporation, with a good, concerned chief executive, becomes the target of a larger—or even smaller—public
corporation, headed by a fast-moving counterpart. This
may have been "dirty stuff" once, particularly for the
prestigious investment bankers, but no longer. In fact
some of the best and brightest are now creatively broker-
ing these raids. Some even introduce them to, then develop them for, ambitious CEOs. It means that the great
and growing corporation to which you sold may now
become a division itself—and of an entirely different operation, with a different tone and style and maybe an
unpleasant one.

Can you avoid it? Not easily. Your only insurance is
if the corporation you are selling to fully controls its

business. The chief executive officer, his associates, and a number of the directors must own at least working control of the corporation's stock—51 percent or at minimum 20 percent. Unfortunately, many don't. This is why it is better at times to sell to a smaller public corporation, whose key people do, or to an operation in which you yourself will be a major stockholder or among them.

But let's move ahead with our scenario. You finally sold and you are satisfied with the deal. The people higher up, including the divisional executive VP or the VP to whom you report, appear to be top quality, the kind you enjoy working with. They were no-nonsense types premerger, are fair now, and they are not nitpickers. They even compromised in a few important areas, which made the deal possible for you. Fine—but. . . .

You are beginning to realize you made one mistake. You accepted a $100,000 salary for each of the five years of your contract. Yes, you requested annual increments to raise you to $150,000 yearly, but you were talked out of it, on the basis of your $90,000 worth of stock dividends. In fact, you were given the impression, subtly, that your dividends might soon increase. It was also explained that your $100,000 was consistent with if not better than the salaries for other managers on your level in the corporation. Finally, and in such a friendly way, you were told that if your performance warranted, your annual stipend might increase without asking. Weren't you placed in the corporation's profit-sharing program? It was not mentioned that this was in lieu of your own very good retirement plan, which in the long run could have been better for you—but no matter. You wanted to complete the deal, and amicably, so you rationalize your one mistake. And you hope. . . .

Now, what do you want in the coming five years? Do you want to stick with your present business, or rise in the hierarchy to corporate VP, executive VP, and onto the board? If so, how do you go about it?

Again back to the bottom line. You are running a profit center and you have to show profit, continuously, year after year. Sales must grow too, and that means more of your energies must go into greater marketing and sales effort, and into product innovation. If so, you will probably be elected a corporate VP in about three years, with greater authority but greater responsibility too, which in turn could win you further promotions, more authority, still greater responsibility. It might even protect you in a raid.

What else is expected of you? A lot. You'll have to blend with the corporate profile, show you *belong* to the corporate hierarchy. You probably won't have to become a yes man, but your own business philosophy must complement the corporation's. You will have to have at least a few original, but always acceptable, ideas to help corporate growth—always consistent with policy, of course. What is good for the corporation must, to other eyes and your own, appear good for you.

Don't however try to become close, personal friends with your chief executive officer, president, or top echelon executives. Cordial yes, but buddy-buddy no—absolutely not. The same for your wife in her dealings with other women in the hierarchy. You and your wife will be invited out socially, on special occasions, and how you both behave will bear heavily on your future.

But nothing is more important than your bottom line. You will have to adjust to new forms of budgeting, to reporting, and to five-year projections. You may think these things are nonsense. Don't let yourself. They are integral to the corporate financial picture. If you are oriented to accounting and have some ideas how to improve these procedures, offer them to the corporate budgeting group. Otherwise, just listen and do what they say. It can be helpful to your profit center, and thus to you. If you don't like it, adjust quickly.

Should you go on the board of your parent corporation? Because today's trend is toward outside directors—as many or more on the board than the number of corporate or divisional executives—you probably won't be invited. Do not feel disappointed. Being a corporate board member, especially for an insider, is just so much window dressing and it has disadvantages too. Chances are you wouldn't have much clout anyway, and if you asked too many questions, or pointed ones, you would be cut down. The boards of most big public companies are usually run by the executive committee and normally the chief executive officer calls most of the shots. Unless it's crucial to your rise, and unless rising is what you want, stay off.

Of course, we could rewrite this scenario a different way. Maybe you will hate every minute of your new life, or be unable or unwilling to adjust to the corporation's needs or to what it expects of you as president or manager of a profit center. You will just have to sweat out those five years the best you can, or ask to be relieved of your new responsibility. If your bottom line is below corporate expectations, that problem will be solved for you. It would mean a contract settlement, freeing you of the corporation and the corporation of you, and it can happen without acrimony.

Finally, remember that the average business life of the entrepreneur-executive is two to three years from the merger date. Still, under exceptional circumstances a few exceptional people have made it big, and once in a while one does become chief executive officer. It depends on who you are, what you want, the corporation you merge with, the people who run it, and what they think of you. On all that, yes, but also on your own ability, and above all on your bottom line. It's the only way the merger game is played.

Appendix

Legal Aspects, Accounting Requirements, and Tax Options

No MERGER or acquisition can be made without a lawyer, but dealing with lawyers in such situations is not simple. Lawyers have their own language, which even other lawyers have difficulty understanding. Thus, unless you know legalese, you may be in for real trouble. The way out is to ask your attorney to interpret, elucidate, explicate—to put legalese into plain English.

Some people say they have such confidence in their attorney that there's no reason to become involved themselves in legal matters. They just sign whatever is put in front of them. This is a mistake. Sure, you have confidence in your lawyer, but you cannot give him a blank check. You do not have to be a lawyer yourself to read a contract, or at least to learn what is in it. Remember, whatever is in the contract you sign is something you alone have to live with—not your lawyer. What must you do to protect yourself, to make sure you are getting what you expect in your merger?

Use your own lawyer if he's qualified for this kind of work, or engage someone else better qualified who comes to you highly recommended. He should be a capable corporate attorney with experience in the merger game. He should be a fine human being, patient and understanding, a person you have confidence in. He should have special skill in writing contracts, and be able to work effectively and creatively with your accountant, particularly on tax matters.

The procedures and laws for mergers and consolidations are covered by the business corporation laws of the state or states where the merging corporations are incorporated, not where the businesses are located. Let's look at the laws of one state, New York, as an example.

Section 901 defines the difference between a merger and a consolidation. A merger is when two or more corporations join with an existing corporation, which is also a party in the merger. A consolidation takes place when two or more corporations join to form a new corporation.

The procedure for implementing a merger or consolidation is found in Section 902. The board of directors of each corporation first approves a Plan of Merger or Consolidation. Among other things the plan sets forth the classes of stock issued and outstanding, and which class has voting rights, and the terms and conditions of the proposed merger or consolidation, including the manner and basis of the exchange of shares, or the cash or other considerations to be paid for the shares.

Section 903 governs stockholder authorization. After the directors have adopted the merger plan it is submitted to stockholders. A copy of the plan must be sent to each stockholder with a notice of meeting, and the plan must be adopted by two-thirds of the shareholders entitled to vote. Each class of voting stock must also approve the plan by vote of two-thirds of the outstanding stock of that class. After the plan is adopted by the board and approved by the stockholders, the attorneys prepare the certificate of merger and file it with the Department of State.

Sections 909 and 910 refer to an asset deal for cash, stock, or other consideration. They provide that no right of appraisal may be had by a dissenting stockholder if the consideration is to be cash, and if the net assets will be distributed within one year under the Plan of Merger. In almost all other cases, a dissenting stockholder is entitled to appraisal rights if he does not believe he is receiving fair value for his shares.

Among the attorney's various duties in an acquisition is to review all basic documents of the acquiring company, as well as the company to be acquired. This is called a "legal audit." The purpose is to make sure there will be no unexpected problems later. This work must be done before the deal is consummated and will determine the answers to these questions:

1. Are the corporation's actions authorized? That is,

are there enough authorized shares to effectuate the transaction; is stockholder approval required, etc.? Applicable preferred stock provisions and indenture provisions should be reviewed.

2. Are there any corporate and loan agreements that impose restrictions on an acquisition, anything that specifically prohibits the action or requires the acquiring company to maintian certain financial ratios?

3. Are leases automatically assumable by the acquiring company, or is consent of a landlord required? If land and buildings are involved, real estate taxes, transfer taxes, title insurance, and the like must all be reviewed.

4. Are there problems with union agreements? Are the agreements for one company compatible with those covering the other? Have you looked at severance or accrued vacation pay?

5. What about your exposure to unfunded liabilities of pension and profit-sharing plans? Should your plan be merged with theirs or terminated?

6. Have you considered antitrust laws, or any consent decrees that may be outstanding? Pending litigation? Will the transaction be attacked under antitrust, SEC, or other laws by the stockholders of either the acquiring or the acquired entity?

7. Are finder's fees payable? How was the transaction brought about, and are there laws stipulating that all finder's agreements be in writing?

8. What are the rights of dissenting stockholders? For example, if more than 10 percent of the stockholders dissent, either company may want to terminate the

agreement. The number of dissenting shares is significant. It bears on preserving a tax loss, ensuring the applicability of pooling of interest accounting (if that is required), and also has implications for basic cash-flow needs that will arise.

9. Can you get hold of the financial statements of the company to be acquired? SEC requirements may make it necessary to have certified financial statements of the acquired company going back three years. The cost of developing them, if they are not available, must be considered.

10. What will be the content and timing of announcements, and who will issue them? Consult with stock-exchange listing representatives. If indentures are outstanding, confirm the continuing eligibility of the trustee under the Trust Indenture Act.

11. Have you reviewed all documents filed over the last five years with any governmental agency, particularly the SEC, both for the information they contain and to ensure completeness and accuracy? Will it be necessary to prepare current reports on SEC Form 8-K, a 13-D statement (where more than 5 percent of the stock of the company is changing hands and it is not a merger), a 14-F statement (where, pursuant to the transfer of securities, the board of directors of a company will change without a vote of stockholders)?

12. Have you considered the short-swing profit provisions of Securities Exchange Act Section 16? Review this as it bears upon options and warrants. This becomes significant if any of the affiliates of the acquired company

become affiliates of the acquiring company, such as members of the board of directors or 10 percent of the stockholders.

13. If the acquisition is by sale of stock, and only a portion of the outstanding stock of the acquired company is involved, have you examined state law provisions relating to premiums for sale of control? Consider the advisability of a tender to the minority of stockholders.

14. Are you aware that, in any event, the provisions of Rule 10b-5 under the Securities Exchange Act will be applicable? There must be full and accurate disclosure of all material facts. The provisions of Rule 10b-5 apply even when the acquired or acquiring company is private. It has been used frequently when certain principals of a private company acquired stock from the remaining principals, while negotiations were pending with an unaffiliated acquiring company. Upon completing the acquisition, the principals who sold their stock to the other principals have contended, successfully, that they should have been advised of the pending negotiations.

Let's look more closely at what mergers are and the forms they can take. Here are a few:

1. In a technical merger, one corporation merges into a second under applicable state laws. Here, dissenting stockholders have appraisal rights. It is also interesting that unless specifically reserved at the time of the merger, representations and warranties effectively terminate. This means no obligations of the merged company continue, unless individual officers, directors, or stock-

holders have personally agreed to indemnify the surviving company. Such indemnifications are common and could survive the merger for an agreed-upon period, usually six months to three years.

Also a technical merger, a corporation will merge into a subsidiary of a parent company, with the stockholders receiving the parent's shares. This happens frequently, especially when a diversified public company prefers to put an acquisition into one of its subsidiaries whose business is more closely related than the parent's. Sometimes it forms a new subsidiary specifically for that purpose. In that case, the merged company will operate autonomously, with its own budgets, staff, and so forth. This can be desirable from the seller's viewpoint and sometimes from the buyer's. This type of merger is also effective when a parent company wants the merged company and its chief executive to assume operations of its subsidiary, particularly when the acquired company is larger, more important, perhaps even more profitable than the subsidiary.

A third type of technical merger, becoming more popular, is one in which a company is acquired and its stockholders (or owners) are paid cash, not stock in the parent company. Cash payments themselves are not really new. What is new is the technique and objective to "force" minority stockholders of the acquired company to relinquish their equity positions. This proved especially useful in closely held, private companies, whose minority stockholders or lesser partners objected strongly to taking stock, or to losing what they believed had been their important position with the company.

2. Another transaction, sometimes called a merger but technically not, is the stock-for-stock deal. For it to work, all stockholders of the acquired company must agree to it.

3. Also interesting is a deal in which stock of the acquiring company is issued for the assets of the acquired. Here, as in stock-for-stock transactions, dissenting stockholders may not get appraisal rights, if payment will be cash and the seller's net assets will be distributed in one year. As a practical matter, however, dissenting stockholders will rarely avail themselves of appraisal rights because of the costs and the difficulties involved. It may also be necessary to comply with bulk sales laws in this transaction. The asset-for-stock arrangement also protects the acquiring company from undisclosed or hidden liabilities.

4. Or, in another transaction type, a company may divest itself of a division for either cash or stock. The acquiring company will obtain an autonomous business, or part of one, and will then make it a self-contained operation, or part of its existing business.

In any of these deals, the consideration to be paid to the sellers may be increased, depending upon future events such as the performance of the acquired company or the market value of the shares acquired in the transaction. Some things on this to think about:

1. Is the consideration determined by or contingent on future events? Often, future performance of the ac-

quired company—the earn-out—is figured into the purchase price. Further, if stockholders of the acquired company receive shares in the acquiring company, the number they get could increase if the market price drops as of predetermined dates. This offers downside risk protection, and was popular during the late sixties and early seventies. However, it turned out that acquiring companies were exposed badly during the precipitous markets in those years, with the result that principals of acquired companies wound up with large chunks of the parent's stock. From the acquired's viewpoint this sort of thing was good—unless the parent went bankrupt (in which case these provisions were terminated by the court), or if the parent placed heavy charges or limitations on the acquired company's operations. However, when the acquiring company was anxious to retain the goodwill of the acquired's principals or keep a good management intact, the earn-out succeeded.

2. Have ramifications been reviewed, such as compliance with IRS continuity-of-interest provisions to ensure a tax-free exchange? Consider the importance of eliminating appraisal rights, the practicalities of obtaining requisite stockholder approvals.

3. Have you observed applicable SEC requirements? Get your accountants and lawyers together on this. It's important.

Let's look at the accounting requirements in a merger or sale. The corporation president is rarely an accountant, yet to manage a business effectively he must know something about accounting, if only to use his accounting officer properly. It is vital to get the best, most professional, accounting talent you can, within your company and outside it. A lot has happened here too since the sixties, the days when accountants were supercreative, shall we say, and as charismatic as their go-go conglomerating clients. Since then the rules have changed, but the fact remains, good accounting is the best insurance a manager can buy.

Two phrases that your accountants will be using in your merger or acquisition situation will be "pooling of interests" and "purchase." You have heard them bandied about, but what, precisely, do they mean?

Trying to say it simply, pooling of interests takes place when the common stock shareholders of two or more businesses—yours and the corporation you re merging with—combine interests and continue as shareholders of the joined enterprise. (This, of course, is a merger and not a sale: neither company purchases the other.) The rule is that the carrying value, based upon historical cost, of all balance sheet accounts is brought forward to the books of the successor corporation, as if the constituent companies had always been one. A purchase is different. In a purchase, one company's shareholders terminate, or significantly modify, their equity interest in the combined company. The result is that the assets of the acquired company are restated to reflect the fair value to the acquiring company.

It is important that if you wish to emphasize the income statement, rather than the balance sheet, a pooling of interests may be more favorable. This result is due to the absence of subsequent charges to the income statement relative to the increment in the booked value of the assets, including the amortization of goodwill.

The accounting rules for business combinations, in force during the sixties, were contained in Accounting Research Bulletin No. 48, issued in January 1957 by the Committee on Accounting Procedure, the predecessor of the Accounting Principles Board, and the grandfather of the present Financial Accounting Standards Board. Merger-expert accountants say these rules were not complex (or not for them), and had they not been abused in practice (as they were) they would probably have stayed intact. Anyway, pooling of interests is so complicated that the American Institute of Certified Public Accounts published a detailed analysis of it in APB Opinion No. 16. Here are a few paragraphs that may—or may not—help you understand it:

POOLING OF INTERESTS METHOD: the pooling of interests method accounts for a business combination as the uniting of the ownership interests of two or more companies by exchange of equity securities. No acquisition is recognized because the combination is accomplished without disbursing resources of the constituents. Ownership interests continue and the former bases of accounting are retained. The recorded assets and liabilities of the constituents are carried forward to the combined corporation at their recorded amounts. Income of the combined corporation includes income of the constituents for the entire fiscal period in which the combination occurs. The reported income of the constituents for prior periods is combined and restated as income of the combined corporation.

The original concept of pooling of interests as a fusion of equity interests was modified in practice as use of the method expanded. The method was first applied in accounting for combinations of affiliated corporations and then extended to some combinations of unrelated corporate ownership interests of comparable size. The method was later accepted for most business combinations in which common stock was issued. New and complex securities have been issued in recent business combinations and some combinations are accounted for as poolings of interests. Some combinations effected by both disbursing cash and issuing securities are now accounted for as a "part purchase, part pooling."

Some accountants believe that the pooling of interests method is the only acceptable method for a combination which meets the requirements for pooling. Others interpret the existing pronouncements on accounting for business combinations to mean that a combination which meets the criteria for a pooling of interests may alternatively be accounted for as a purchase.

Accounting Research Bulletin No. 48 also suggested there should be management continuity as well. Included too was a "size test," calling for a disparity no greater than 90 to 95 percent between the combining entities. The Bulletin proposed that in the year a pooling of interests occurred, the operating statements for the entire year were to be combined. However, the problem with ARB 48 was that it was too wishy-washy. According to the accounting profession, it used such terms as "may," "tends to indicate," and "presumption," instead of setting hard and fast rules, with the result that the criteria for pooling deteriorated through benign interpretations of their meaning. For example:

In 1967 one of the semiautonomous subsidiaries of a well-known corporation, based in Texas, acquired a sizable and profitable company for $22 million of the subsidiary's common stock and $5 million cash. In addition, and directly contravening ARB 48's paragraph five ("there cannot be a plan to dispose of a substantial amount of the stock received"), the shareholders of the acquired company got the right to have 80 percent of the stock they received registered at the expense of the acquiring subsidiary within four months of the combination, with the parent guaranteeing a selling price of $22.22 per share. Later these stockholders exercised their right to "put" their shares, at about the same time as the financial statements (accounting for the transaction as a pooling of interests) were issued. The company did not even treat the transaction as part pooling, part purchase (to the extent of the cash involved), another gambit that became popular because ARB 48 did not prohibit it.

Another corporation, a noted conglomerate of the 1960s, acquired a large insurance company in 1968, paying with $400 million in cash, preferred stock, and warrants. Because this transaction was accounted for as a pooling, the assets of the insurance company were booked by the conglomerate at $171 million, the historical cost to the insurance company. Included in the assets was a portfolio of marketable securities with a cost of $111 million and a market value of $250 million. Obviously, the $400 million purchase price took into account the market value of the securities. The following year, 1969, the conglomerate reported a $24 million profit on the sale of some of the securities, nearly 60 percent of its total net income for the year. Although the market value of the portfolio was down in that year by $58 million, by selling a piece of it the conglomerate could beef up its profits, also down. It simply sold appreciated assets after the merger and showed the profits as net income.

Another practice in that era was to combine the statements of companies that pooled after their fiscal closings, but before the statements were released. The justification was that, when a pooling occurs, it is just as if the companies were always one. If a conglomerate had not had a hot year, had not shown the growth everyone expected, it merely pooled in a profitable company before the statements were issued. Some conglomerates even had a list of such profitable companies ready and waiting, a reserve much like the old taxi squads in pro football. Because ARB 48 did not insist that prior-year statements reflect the effects of a pooling, many of these highflyers did not restate, and instead issued misleading financials. Finally the Accounting Principle Board put a stop to this. In December 1966 it issued ABP Opinion No. 10, requiring that all statements presented for comparative purposes be restated to show the effects of a later pooling.

The term "purchase accounting" was not so clear either during the go-go years. In many instances the acquiring company booked the acquisition cost of the assets it purchased, at book value to the seller, and entered the excess as goodwill. Goodwill at that time was not amortized against earnings. As long as the acquired company was profitable, it could be carried on the books forever.

Thus in August 1970 the Accounting Principle Board issued opinions 16 and 17. Their thrust was to stop these abusive practices, to make sure that combinations that qualified for pooling maintained the pooling spirit. In doing so the board defined the following:

1. Attributes of the "combining companies":

a. Each must be autonomous and must not have been a subsidiary or a division of another corporation for two years preceding the initiation of the plan of combination (a new company organized during this two-year period meets the autonomy test). The APB felt this provision was necessary to assure consistency with the underlying pooling concept: independent shareholders combining their interests. No such transaction could take place with a subsidiary or a division of another company.

b. Each of the combining companies is independent of the other. No more than a 10 percent of ownership relationship is permitted. Although the 10 percent figure is arbitrary and probably represents a compromise, it prevents companies from pooling with themselves, the theory being that in many public companies 10 percent is a controlling interest. The acquisition of a minority interest must be accounted for as a purchase.

2. Mode of "combining of interest":

a. The combination must be effected in a single transaction, or be completed within one year, pursuant to a specific plan. Altering the terms of an exchange of stock means a new plan. If the plan is delayed because of governmental intervention or other litigation, the one-year rule is waived.

b. The acquiring corporation offers and issues only common stock, whose rights are identical to the rights of the majority shareholders of its outstanding voting common stock. No more preferred stock warrants or other "funny money." However, the acquiring corporation may purchase up to 10 percent of the acquired company's shares for cash. The cash cannot be spread among the shareholders, except for some small amounts, but must go only to dissenting shareholders.

c. Extraordinary distributions are prohibited before a combination. A combining company cannot put cash in the hands of its shareholders by paying an unusual dividend prior to the combination.

d. Treasury stock may not be unduly accumulated by the acquiring company within two years of the plan of combination. The theory is that you cannot have a pooling when you pay cash. Therefore, a company cannot buy back its outstanding common stock with cash, then use this new treasury stock for an acquisition. Treasury stock acquisitions are allowed for stock option plans, however, and for other combinations to be accounted for as purchases, or for contingency arrangements under previous combinations.

e. The "ratio of interest" among common shareholders must be preserved. That is, each shareholder must end up with the same proportionate interest in the combined company as he had in one company before the combination.

f. Voting rights of the newly issued shares are exercisable immediately. Voting trusts are out. These were used extensively in past combinations, mainly to prevent losing control of a public company when a large amount of stock was issued for a combination.

g. The combination must be resolved on the date the plan is consummated to eliminate contingent or escrowed shares. This too was common earlier. There were provisions to issue additional shares if profits of the acquired company reached a certain level, or if the market value of the issued stock declined.

3. Absence of certain "planned transactions":

a. The combined corporation may not retire or reacquire any of the newly issued shares. In substance this would result in the issuance of cash, which is prohibited.

b. The combined corporation must not enter into a "financial arrangement" favoring any of the shareholders of the acquired company (say, to give them a "guaranteed take out" or a "put" option). However, the shareholders may arrange on their own to sell their securities. In ASR 135 the SEC says they must wait for a financial statement of the combined company covering at least 30 days of operations.

c. The combined corporation does not intend, or plan, to dispose of a significant part of the assets of the combining companies within two years after the combination, other than in the ordinary course of business or to eliminate duplicate facilities or excess capacity. This provision prohibits the fabrication of instant profits, as often occurred under the old rules.

Basically, the accounting for pooling is this: The assets, liabilities, and shareholders' equities of the constituent companies are combined at their former cost. A pooling that occurs during the year results in a combined statement for the entire year, and reflects earlier years for comparative purposes. The new opinion, like most APB pronouncements, requires additional disclosures, such as the name and brief description of the company pooled, that the transaction has been accounted for under the pooling of interest method, a description of shares, and the number issued in the combination. Also reflected should be the results of each company's operations before the combination. These would be such items as revenue, extraordinary items, net income, other changes in shareholders' equity accounts, and amount and manner of accounting for intercompany transactions.

A pooling of interests that takes place after the fiscal year has ended, but before financials are issued, no longer affects the year just closed. The pooling, however, may be disclosed as supplemental information, usually in a footnote setting forth the effects of the combination on the reported financial position and the results of operations.

Finally, the opinion requires that costs of the combination, including legal, accounting, finder's fees, registration expenses, and the like, must be charged to current net income, not to paid-in capital as they once were.

It is also important that if the combination does not qualify as a pooling of interest, it is accounted for as a purchase interest. The net assets of the acquired company are recorded by the purchaser at fair values for the transaction. The operations of the acquired companies are combined only from the date of acquisition, and prior periods cannot be restated except as supplemental data. If the purchase is for cash, for assets, or by incurring liabilities, the cost is readily determinable. On the other hand, if capital stock or the like is issued, there is an evaluation problem. A fair value of the purchase must be determined. Simply relying on the quoted market value of the stock (if it is publicly traded) is not sufficient. Once the total value of the consideration has been established, it should be apportioned among the assets acquired. For example, the inventory value is based upon the expected selling price, less a reasonable profit for selling, not upon the cost to the acquired company. Independent appraisals are also required to establish the values of some of the assets, particularly property, plant, and equipment involved. Remember that a fair value of the assets could exceed the total cost of the company. The result is what accountants refer to as "negative goodwill."

Let's turn to the tax options and possibilities of a merger. Although the subject is complicated and technical, only two basic tax options exist: a taxable sale, which involves a capital gains treatment, or a tax-free sale, which has several variations.

A taxable sale of a business is (1) a sale solely for cash, or (2) a sale for a combination of cash and notes. The first is self-explanatory, but item two needs some elaboration.

When a company is sold for cash, the IRS is quite explicit. You must pay a capital gains tax, whatever it happens to be at the time of sale. Not too many years ago it was 25 percent; today it can run as high as 50 percent. Remember, an all-cash deal is not a merger. It is a sale.

Although the simplest and easiest way to dispose of a business in a taxable transaction is by cash through a certified check, the Tax Reform Act of 1976 suggests that an all-stock deal may now be preferable. It is important to remember that the Tax Reform Act of 1976 has put an additional crimp on capital gains, bringing new rules into the merger game from this special vantage point. Still more tightening will be in evidence in future "reform" tax legislation. This will mean more dilution of the benefits from long-term capital gains. *C'est la vie.*

Now to return to the sale of a business in a taxable transaction for cash through a certified check. In this type of transaction, the seller will do well to make certain that the stock he receives is not restricted, or only slightly. The seller should have the option to sell any portion of the stock he receives for his company (or for the stock of his company) as soon after the merger transaction as possible—certainly no later than six months to a year. Of course, he will lose this option automatically if he accepts election to the board of directors of the buying corporation. He is then an "insider" and the disposal of his stock becomes subject to SEC rules. Also, the buyer must be certain (as best he can) that the corporation with which he merges, and whose stock he receives, is rock solid. It is essential to evaluate thoroughly its financial statements, including annual and 10-K reports, and the corporation's ten-year record. Look closely for fluctuations in the price of the stock of the corporation over a period of time, as well as its P/E.

Selling for cash and notes, to qualify for installment sale treatment, is a little more complex. The purpose of this method is to provide the seller (an individual, an entrepreneur, or a closely held family company) with a capital gain. At the same time it makes it possible for the buyer to extend the payments for the acquired business over a period of time, usually five years.

It is important to remember that in a cash-and-notes transaction, the seller may not receive more than 30 percent of the selling price in the taxable year of the sale (Internal Revenue Code, section 453.) If the seller accepts more than 30 percent in cash, he will be required to pay a tax on the entire transaction when he files his tax return for that year. The entire amount will become taxable in the year of the sale, even though the seller has only received a portion of the sale proceeds. However, if he follows the law to the letter, accepting no more than 30 percent in cash at the time of the closing, he pays a capital gains tax only when he actually receives payment. Thus a five-year payout lets him defer taxes, paying for his gains as he receives them.

It is also important to remember that under the 1976 Tax Reform Act, long-term capital gains could have an adverse effect upon a person's maximum tax rate on salary. This is another element that should be considered seriously in determining whether to sell a business on an installment basis. For example, if you are a high-salaried individual you may be better off to take the entire proceeds in one year, rather than over an extended period. If your annual salary is $200,000 and you report a long-term capital gain of $2 million, and if you take the entire capital gain in one year, you will receive the benefit of a 25 percent tax applied to the first $50,000 of capital gains—but your salary will be taxed at 70 percent, not 50 percent. However, if you received $2 million in long-term capital gains and if your annual salary is $200,000, and if you spread gains over five years, your salary will be taxed at 70 percent *during each of those five years*. Obviously you would be better off taking the long-term capital gains in one year.

Naturally, there is no reason for the seller of a business to pay more taxes than is legally necessary. Fortunately, several tax-free options are available.

The most common option involves the sale of assets for stock, or of stock for other stock. In each case the exchange involves only the voting stock (usually the common) of the purchasing corporation. This is all highly technical, but your accountant and lawyer will understand it.

Drawing up a contract in a stock-for-stock transaction is simpler than for an assets-for-stock transaction. In the latter, every asset and every liability of the seller's corporation must be listed, specifically and carefully. It is essential to watch for a failure to list all liabilities. Should this happen, the seller becomes liable for them himself. That is why the buyer usually requires that a portion of the stock he gives the seller be held in escrow for a number of years, until all liabilities are accounted for, or none are found. If unrecorded liabilities are discovered, the seller forfeits a number of his shares, the amount depending on the amount of the liabilities. This can be quite substantial. Although there is no reason for liabilities to be unrecorded, some can be overlooked. And, although a portion of the stock he is to receive for his business is being withheld in escrow, the seller is normally required to pay the escrow charges. It may not amount to much, but it is another cost for the seller.

And here is an interesting twist. In a disposition by merger, the seller can receive voting stock tax-free. Cash added is taxable, usually as ordinary income. This type of sale may prove desirable for the seller, who may want cash as well as stock, but who worries about the tax consequences. If the cash portion is small, about 10 percent of the total transaction or less, it may be the thing to do, certainly for the seller whose assets are mainly in his business.

Index